STILL STANDING

LEADING WELL-BEING IN CRISIS-TESTED HEALTHCARE SYSTEMS

What do we do after the storm clears,
but the damage is still inside us?

Laurinda Calongne, EdD
Foreword by Gigi Dunn, MD

The content of this book is based on personal and professional reflections and is not intended as medical, legal, or psychological advice. This content is for educational and inspirational use only and does not replace professional advice. Although efforts have been made to provide accurate information, the author does not guarantee the completeness, reliability, or suitability of the material presented.

The author's stories and examples come from healthcare experience and observation. Some details have been altered for privacy. The intent is to honor the complexity of real events while preserving the integrity of the lessons they offer.

ISBN 979-8-9935920-0-8 (Paperback)

ISBN 979-8-9935920-1-5 (Ebook)

Book and ebook design by Indira McGuire, Butter Designs
Cover design by Erika Duran

Independently published Standing Strong Strategies LLC
Printed in the United States of America

Dedication

For Dan,

Thank you for being my constant, my encourager, and my home.
I am blessed beyond measure to walk this life with you.

Table of Contents

Acknowledgments

Many people have crossed my professional path over the years, and I wish I could thank each one by name. Every conversation, collaboration, and shared experience has shaped the lens through which I view this work.

I especially want to recognize those who have been instrumental in advising, supporting, and guiding my work in healthcare well-being and systemic cultural change.

Much of my work in cross-institutional and national initiatives has only been possible because of the deep engagement, commitment, and vision of these organizations:

- The Alliance of Independent Academic Medical Centers (AIAMC)
- Accreditation Council on Graduate Medical Education (ACGME)
- American Medical Association (AMA)
- American Hospital Association (AHA)

Their leadership in this space has been foundational. Their willingness to move beyond checklists and compliance—and into meaningful conversations about human sustainability in medicine—has been essential to the evolution of this work.

To my colleagues who stepped up when it was not easy, when burnout was still viewed by many as a personal weakness rather than a systemic warning sign, thank you for your partnership, honesty, and courage: Dr. Shannon Alwood, Dr. Curtis Chastain, Dr. Kathleen Crapanzano, Dr. Jimmy Craven, Dr. Gigi Dunn, Dr. Kelly Finan, Dr. Steven Gremillion, Mr. Peter Guarisco, Dr. London Guidry, Tanya Haase, Dr. Laura Hetzler, Dr. Angie Johnson, Dr. Dean Lauret, Dr. Kevin Reed, Dr. Melissa Roy, Dr. Keith Rhynes, Dr. Chris Thomas, Dr. Nicole Telhiard, Rich Vath, LaDonna Williams, and Dr. Karen Williams.

Your belief in this work and the importance of caring for our people, not just our patients, gave this movement momentum when needed.

Finally, thank you for your trust and support from Mr. John Finan and Mr. Scott Wester, whose executive leadership allowed this work to take root in a system that was not always ready for it. Doing this kind of work in healthcare requires conviction and cover. Your leadership made a difference.

This book stands on the shoulders of many. I appreciate each of you.

—Laurinda

Foreword

As an anesthesiologist who spent two decades in the operating room, I know what it means to show up for patients in critical circumstances when they are most vulnerable — and to lead teams through pressure that leaves no room for error. I also know the toll that cumulative trauma, moral distress, and burnout can take on the people who keep our healthcare systems running.

Dr. Laurinda Calongne understands this, too, but in a truly rare way. She brings to *Still Standing* a perspective shaped both by her years as a trauma-trained clinician and her service as a C-suite healthcare executive. She has stood in the ER with grieving families and in boardrooms making decisions that would shape the future of entire health systems. This unique advantage gives her an uncommon ability to bridge the deep human reality of frontline care with the strategic foresight required to lead systemic change.

In my journey from being a board-certified anesthesiologist and physician leader, through fellowship training in integrative medicine, to certification in traumatic stress studies, I have met many leaders who speak about resilience. Far too few understand that resilience without recovery is unsustainable. Laurinda is one of those few. She recognizes that sustainable healthcare requires cultures valuing both healing and performance, as well as recovery and resilience.

What you will find in these pages is not theory or distant observation. Laurinda offers stories that are raw and real, drawn from hurricanes, floods, pandemics, and the everyday grind of healthcare work in high-pressure environments. She combines stories with actionable strategies for creating healthcare systems where people can serve, survive, and thrive.

Laurinda's work is based on the often-unspoken reality in healthcare: burnout is not a personal weakness. It is a symptom of systemic dysfunction. It is the red warning light on the dashboard, telling us that the system is operating beyond safe limits. Just as a responsible driver would not ignore that warning light, a responsible leader cannot ignore the signs of exhaustion, depletion, and moral injury in their workforce.

Still Standing is as much a call to action as it is a blueprint. It urges leaders to stop viewing burnout as a personal issue fixable by time off. The recommendation is to establish workplaces that consider well-being as an essential factor and recognize recovery needs.

In my work, I have seen how trauma and moral injury can erode not only individual lives but also the culture of entire healthcare organizations. Left unaddressed, they create an undercurrent of fear, mistrust, and disengagement. This leads to downstream impacts on clinical outcomes and institutional stability. However, I have also seen what Laurinda describes here: with educated and intentional leadership, recovery is possible. Teams can reconnect. Trust can be re-established. It is possible to restore and strengthen the human component within a healthcare system.

This book offers both the why and the how. Laurinda's "why" comes from lived experience: decades of seeing colleagues carry grief and trauma in silence, of witnessing heroism misused as an excuse to demand more from those already at their limit. Her "how" is rooted in proven approaches to trauma-informed leadership, system-wide, evidence-based wellness initiatives led by those with specialty training, and cultural change. The combination is powerful — and urgently needed.

Healthcare does not need another push to work harder. It requires permission and structure to heal through initiatives that reach every facet of the institution. It requires leaders who can recognize when the tank is empty and know how to refill it. Systems must realize that people's well-being is essential for patient safety, quality, and sustainability.

Read this book with an open mind, but more importantly, with a willingness to act. Laurinda's insights will validate what so many have felt but have not had the words to express. They will challenge you to examine culture and leadership practices within your healthcare system. Furthermore, they will equip you with concrete steps to begin building something better.

For every healthcare professional who has sat in their car after a shift, too tired to drive home, for every leader who has wondered how to protect their people from breaking under the weight of constant crisis, and for every student just starting their journey in this field — *Still Standing* offers hope, clarity, and a path forward.

Laurinda reminds us that survival is not enough; the real goal is to design systems that integrate healing and innovation, making space for caregivers to be whole.

— Gigi Dunn, MD
Board-Certified Anesthesiologist and Physician Executive
Fellowship-Integrative Medicine:
University of Arizona College of Medicine,
Andrew Weil Center for Integrative Medicine
Traumatic Stress Certification-Trauma Research Foundation
Advocate for Trauma-Informed Healthcare Transformation

PREFACE
Why I Wrote This Book

I had always had a well-stocked toolkit: years **in** high-intensity settings and a stubborn commitment to well-being. I had weathered storms before. During the COVID-19 pandemic, something shifted.

At a meeting in Chicago, my elbow began to swell and throb. My colleagues advised me to have a checkup before I flew home. At a walk-in clinic, a nurse asked for a urine sample, and I realized I had not urinated in two days. Lab work revealed I had developed rhabdomyolysis—a dangerous condition where damaged muscle tissue breaks down and releases proteins and electrolytes into the bloodstream, overwhelming the kidneys and sometimes the liver. Mine were already struggling to keep up. Although this condition can result from multiple factors, in my situation, pronounced dehydration was identified as the only significant risk factor. I spent several days in the hospital and experienced significant exhaustion afterward. For the first time, I could not simply push through it.

Months later, a new curveball arrived: a rhythmic whooshing in my ear. During a meeting with my close friend, Dr. Phillip Allen, an ear, nose, and throat specialist, I followed him back to his office for a quick exam, assuming it was just water from a recent beach trip. Instead, after a brief look, he immediately referred me to his colleagues. By the end of the day, I had seen both a neurotologist and a neurosurgeon. The diagnosis was sobering—a temporal bone encephalocele with a cerebrospinal fluid leak. Two days later, at the height of the COVID pandemic, I found myself on the operating table for **brain surgery: a craniotomy and encephalocele repair of the defect.**

People knew me as the one with endless drive, the person who never slowed down, who kept saying *"let us do this"*, who gave until there was nothing left. However, when my body finally broke, I did not get a choice. The damage to my vestibular nerve left me off balance, literally and figuratively. I could not walk a straight line, could not trust my footing. Underneath the dizziness was a more profound exhaustion I could no longer outrun. Stopping was not a decision; it was a collapse. In that quiet, I had to face what I had been avoiding: I was empty. Completely.I had just finished reading *The Body Keeps the Score* by Bessel van der Kolk, and the words echoed painfully—my body was keeping score of two decades spent carrying crisis after crisis. The weight had finally caught up with me.

I had promised myself long ago that I would never cling to a leadership role once I could no longer serve it well. However, this was different. I was not just leaving a job, I was stepping away from something I had poured myself into, something I had built and loved. Letting it go felt like grief. It was as if I had lost a piece of myself, a part of my identity. However, I knew staying would mean giving less than my best, and that was a line I could not cross.

Our health system owns a university, which allowed me to stay close to the mission while shifting my pace. I moved into a faculty role, teaching the next generation of healthcare professionals, and I launched an executive coaching practice, walking alongside leaders in transition. For four years, I was able to rest, reflect, and refocus. I remained rooted in the work I loved—just not at the same relentless speed.

Serving within a Catholic hospital system made the mission personal for me; it was not just an institutional value; it was a calling. Even as I slowed down, I carried that commitment forward. Teaching, mentoring, and coaching became new ways of living out the same mission of care and healing that had always guided me. This work kept tapping me on the shoulder. Client after client named the same ache: burnout, moral distress, a sense that something deeper was off. Organizations tried well-being initiatives. They failed to catch on, not due to apathy, but because our tools were not suited to the challenge. We were treating symptoms.

Prior to my healthcare leadership role, I trained and worked as a clinical social worker in South Louisiana, where hurricanes and floods are not case studies but seasons. Crisis was not abstract; it was Tuesday. Trauma response and critical incident intervention were survival tools in ERs and trauma bays, and I used them every day.

Over the past two decades, I have taught and led national projects focused on well-being. I saw teams recover. I thought I understood what it would take.

Then a respected colleague said, "Until we address burnout through a trauma lens, we are just managing symptoms." It landed harder than I expected. I knew trauma. I had not connected that knowledge to what I was witnessing unfold across clinics, units, and classrooms.

We tend to frame burnout as either a personal weakness or a system failure. Some clinicians have unresolved trauma, and some systems lack resources or processes to address it. When we ignore the trauma under the surface, we mislabel the problem and prescribe the wrong fixes.

That realization is why I authored this book. Not to add another program to a crowded shelf, but to connect what I have lived, on both sides of the bedside, with a way forward.

What follows is the story of how I broke, what I learned as I rebuilt, and how that journey reshaped my leadership. It is also a framework drawn from social work, trauma science, and hard-won lessons in healthcare: practical ways to see what is driving the pain and to respond without causing new harm.

If you recognize yourself in any part of this, you are not alone. I have been the leader who said the wrong thing, the clinician who kept going, the mentor who did not have the right words. I have also watched teams heal when we named what was happening and adjusted how we led.

This preface is not a promise that the road will be easy. It is a simple statement of why I am still here and why this work still matters to me. The introduction maps what you will get and how to use it. For now, I know that there is another way to lead and live in healthcare, and it starts by telling the truth about what we have been through.

—Laurinda Calongne

Introduction

You have kept a unit open with only half the staff needed. You have signed off on plans you did not believe in because there was no other option. The term "resilient" has become widely used, frequently signifying little more than the ability to withstand adversity.

If that is your reality, this book is for you.

What you see is not only burnout, but depletion that persists after a weekend off. It is moral injury that comes from choosing the least harmful option instead of the right one. It is morally distressing to know the right action and to be unable to take it because of constraints. It is unprocessed trauma that sits under the surface of hospitals, clinics, nursing homes, ambulance bays, and classrooms. We have treated symptoms and called it a strategy. We ask people to breathe, hydrate, and check the boxes, then send them back into the same conditions.

This book names the damage and shows you how to build recovery into the work itself, not as an extra program, but as a way of leading. This book offers practical tools for leaders, educators, and clinicians to use in their work. It is not for organizations looking for a poster, a pizza party, or a one-time workshop.

By the end, you will be able to spot depletion early and respond before it becomes attrition. You will know how to build recovery into schedules, staffing, supervision, and daily flow, and how to create small, reliable practices that let teams process grief without leaving the floor. You will also know what to measure, how to talk about it without turning people into dashboards, and how to hold yourself and your leaders to those standards.

If you run a service line, a residency, a unit, a clinic, or a system, you will find tools you can use immediately. If you teach, coach, or precept, you will find language that helps learners name what they carry and move through it. If you are on the floor or in the field, you will see your world reflected and, I hope, feel less alone.

The pattern is the same in both places: we praise resilience and ignore recovery. **Resilience keeps you standing. Recovery keeps you human.**

Here is what to expect in this book:

First, we will tell the truth about what the work has done to us. You will see how disasters, violence, staffing collapse, and daily ethical strain shape people and organizations. You will get a precise, shared vocabulary for burnout, depletion, moral distress, and moral injury.

Next, we will look at the operating system. You will learn what recovery-first leadership looks like in practice: safer staffing ratios such as trauma prevention, supervision that treats humans, not shifts, grief work that fits inside a workday, and policies that reduce harm rather than outsourcing it to the most conscientious person in the room.

Finally, we will cover measurement and momentum. You will learn how to track what matters, make the case to executives, and sustain change after the first wave of enthusiasm fades.

This is a book about people and design. The stories are real, with details changed to protect privacy. Though not perfect, these practices are practical and feasible in real-world settings. Some will expect more from you than ever before. They are worth it. So are your people.

We cannot afford to lose more clinicians, educators, and leaders to preventable burnout. **Resilience without recovery is**

endurance, and endurance runs out. Let us build places where it does not have to.

However, there is another layer to this story—one that starts before the individual is burned out, before the team is short-staffed, and before the leader is weighing which corner to cut. It begins when the next crisis arrives before the last one heals.

That is where we need to start.

1

WHEN THE NEXT CRISIS HITS
Before the Last One Heals

The thing about a crisis is that it rarely announces itself, and it never asks if you are ready. In healthcare, no siren signals when one disaster is over, and another is about to begin. One day, you are rationing PPE in a COVID surge, the next, you are covering blown-out windows after a hurricane. The rhythm is merciless—just enough time to catch half a breath before the next blow lands.

The body adapts, or at least it tries to. Muscles tense at every alert, sleep becomes light and broken, and tempers shorten. Recovery begins to feel like a privilege for someone else. Nurses keep showing up. Physicians keep charting. Environmental services keep cleaning patient rooms. However, behind the motion is the slow realization: survival is different from being well.

I think back to a young surgery resident on his very first day of burn rotation. That day, a mother, father, and two children were pulled from a house fire with third-degree burns covering most of their bodies. None of them survived. The image of their injuries is something I will never forget.

I had grabbed a Coke and a pack of M&Ms, and the resident swiped a whole jar of Skippy peanut butter from the physician's lounge. We sat together in silence, knowing there were no words that could soften what we had just witnessed. We lingered there, side by side, because neither of us was ready for what came next.

That feeling, that impossible question of how to keep showing up in the face of such relentless loss, has never left me. If anything, it has only deepened as crises have piled one on top of another. Some of us break and keep going. Some of us do not.

Four months later, I learned that the resident had committed suicide by hanging himself.

WHEN CRISES COLLIDE

Crises do not respect timelines. Hurricanes do not wait for pandemics to ease. Wildfires do not check hospital staffing grids before they spread. A chemical spill, a mass shooting, or a supply chain collapse can hit just as the workforce is crawling out from the last blow.

Early in the COVID pandemic, many believed a turning point was coming. Cases would fall. Supplies would stabilize. We would finally catch our breath. However, before that moment ever came, another wave arrived. In Louisiana, it was hurricane after hurricane pounding already fragile systems. In other places, there were wildfires, mass shootings, or new surges of infection. The result was the same: recovery time evaporated.

THE HUMAN TOLL

The research is clear: serial crises deepen harm. Four in ten healthcare workers report risk of moral injury. Over 40% develop symptoms of PTSD. Twenty-five percent live with persistent burnout months or even years later (West et al., 2018; Shanafelt & Noseworthy, 2017). These are not sterile numbers. These signs are evident in the fatigued expressions of staff during breaks and in the unfilled positions listed on staffing rosters.

This is not about "stress." Chronic crisis drives allostatic load—the body's biological cost of constant vigilance. In short bursts, adrenaline and cortisol keep us alive. However, when the surge never stops, the system never resets. Blood pressure rises—sleep fractures. Immune defenses weaken. Depression takes root (McEwen, 2004). The toll is cumulative, and eventually, people leave.

Turnover intention, "I am thinking about quitting," spikes after major crises, especially among new nurses, with 36% reporting they plan to exit (NSI Nursing Solutions, 2023). Others quietly step away from healthcare altogether, taking with them years of training and experience that no residency program can replace.

THE SAFETY TOLL

When the workforce is depleted, patients pay the price. Data from Medicare patients during COVID showed a sharp rise in adverse events under surge conditions (Ochieng et al., 2022). Pressure injuries, infections, falls, and preventable pneumonias all climbed. Moreover, those are just the harms we could measure.

The invisible costs are harder to tally: the canceled surgeries, the missed follow-ups, the patients who never make it back until it is too late. The Centers for Disease Control's excess mortality data tells part of the story: lives lost not directly to the crisis itself, but to its aftershocks (Bureau of Labor Statistics, 2023).

THE OPERATIONAL TOLL

Crises strip systems bare. PPE shortages during COVID were only the most visible example. Medication gaps, lab reagent shortages, and missing IV tubing all became life-and-death concerns (U.S. Government Accountability Office, 2021).

Meanwhile, another slow-burning crisis was rising: workplace violence. In 2023, it cost U.S. hospitals over $18 billion (American Hospital Association, 2023). Behind that number are real people: nurses shoved, physicians cursed, technicians threatened by families who were themselves breaking under the weight of fear and grief.

THE EQUITY TOLL

Disasters never fall evenly. Communities with fewer resources lose more access to care. Marginalized workers carry heavier burdens. Recovery funds are frequently allocated based on the prominence of advocacy rather than the severity of need (WHO, 2024; NAM, 2022). Crisis magnifies inequity. Furthermore, back-to-back crises split the cracks wide open.

WHY "SERIAL" IS DIFFERENT

One disaster is manageable—systems rally. Mutual aid kicks in. Given enough time, people heal. However, compound crises—the kind that hit before the last wound closes—shift the trajectory. Damage does not reset; it accumulates (National Academies, 2022).

It is the difference between being knocked down and getting back up versus being hit again while you are still on your knees.

WHAT WORKS

The evidence points to solutions—if we dare to act.

1. **Plan for Overlap, Not Isolation.**

World Health Organization 2024 guidance is clear: design for overlapping crises, not just one-offs. Surge staffing, cross-training, and stockpiles must anticipate multiple disasters at once (WHO, 2024).

2. **Fix the Work Before Asking for More Resilience.**

Self-care cannot cover organizational fractures. Interventions like better staffing ratios, flexible scheduling, and confidential mental health access outperform surface-level wellness fixes (West et al., 2020; NAM, 2022). In serial crises, even evidence-based programs must be adapted: shorter, more targeted, and woven directly into daily workflow.

3. Protect Staff from Violence.

Layered prevention strategies, environmental design, de-escalation training, and reporting systems—reduce violence and its corrosive effect on morale (OSHA, 2023).

4. Close the Recovery Gap.

Recovery is not indulgence; It is clinical safety. Critical incident debriefings should ensure dedicated time for decompression, while recovery monitoring ought to be managed with the same level of rigor as infection control metrics.

THE BOTTOM LINE

Serial crises do not just multiply strain; they transform it. They amplify every vulnerability, including burnout, turnover, patient safety risks, fragile supply chains, and inequities. If resilience remains a motivational slogan, we will lose both our workforce and the safety of our systems.

Resilience must become an operational competency—designed, resourced, and measured. Because in healthcare, the next crisis always hits before the last one heals. The people standing in that gap deserve better than carrying the weight alone.

If the last few years have taught us anything, it is that there is no shortage of effort. Hospitals have launched wellness committees, hired resilience officers, offered yoga sessions, expanded EAP benefits, and rolled out endless variations of "take care of yourself" campaigns.

However, the needle often barely moves. Burnout lingers. Turnover increases. Patient safety slips. Leaders wonder: ***Why aren't things improving despite all our efforts?***

Most of these strategies were not designed for ongoing crises. They assume time to recover, margin to reflect, and stability to rebuild. However, when the next disaster strikes before the last one heals, the usual playbook fails.

This book is intended for organizations and leaders who have recognized this challenge, implemented programs, initiated pilot projects, and dedicated substantial effort, yet continue to face a workforce operating under significant strain. The chapters ahead are meant to answer the questions that linger in those moments:

- What does recovery even look like when the system never gets to rest?
- How do we measure the actual cost of cumulative strain?
- Why do so many interventions fall flat, and what works under sustained pressure?
- What does it mean to lead with both competence and compassion when the crisis never really ends?

I know these questions because I have experienced them. I have participated in boardroom discussions focused on strategic decision-making and have collaborated with colleagues in hospital corridors as we assessed our ability to manage another shift. The demands of exceeding my limits have taken a toll on my health, and my professional journey has been fundamentally altered by the understanding that recovery is essential for continued well-being and effectiveness. This book is the result of those lessons, and it begins with the truth healthcare can no longer afford to ignore.

2

HOW I GOT PULLED INTO THE DEEP END

Trauma, Coping, and the Beginning of a Mission

The page came over the loudspeaker just before noon.

I came back from parental leave early that morning, stepping back into my role as the social worker for the ER at West Jefferson Medical Center. My morning had been a blur of catching up on cases, answering emails, and trying to remember the rhythm of a hospital day after weeks of parental leave. The smells, the constant background noise, the quick pace of hallway conversations all felt both familiar and foreign, like slipping back into a life I had stepped away from but never entirely left behind.

When the ER call came, I walked in expecting the usual. A car accident. An overdose. Instead, the paramedics wheeled in a tiny bundle on a gurney. A two-month-old baby girl is unresponsive.

Her parents were already there. Their sobs cut through the noise of the trauma bay, sharper than any monitor alarm. I froze for a moment that felt longer than it was. She looked so much like my own daughter, Emilie, who was the same age. The resemblance hit me in a way that nothing in my training had prepared me for.

I applied the techniques I learned, maintaining a composed demeanor, attentive presence, and steady communication even during challenging situations. However, it was like moving through water. My voice sounded far away, even to me. My hands were not steady. The world in that room felt too close and too distant all at once.

Later, one of the ER nurses told me they had called my boss to see if another social worker could cover for me. I said no. It was my first day back, we were already short-staffed, and I did not want anyone to think I could not manage it. So, I stayed.

I did my job. Then I carried every bit of it home with me.

That night, I broke down. My mind would not stop replaying what I had seen. I became convinced Emilie might die in her sleep, sure that what I had just witnessed could happen in my own home. We bought every monitor we could find. I moved her crib into our bedroom. For months, I never slept deeply.

At the time, I did not have the language for what I was feeling. I did not know the clinical terms or the frameworks that would later become second nature to me. All I knew was that something inside me had cracked. That day was the first time I understood how thin the line can be between the professional and the personal, between holding it together and falling apart.

That experience did not just rattle me as a new mother; it crystallized something I would come to see often in healthcare: how we absorb trauma silently, how the system rewards stoicism over honesty, and how quickly we learn to mask deep emotional wounds in the name of professionalism.

LEARNING TO BREATHE IN THE DEEP END

That first day back was extreme, but the truth is, I had been in deep water since the start of my career. For the first decade, I was a medical social worker in hospitals across South Louisiana. I began my career at Charity Hospital of New Orleans, serving in one of the nation's most underserved and impoverished communities, an area marked by some of the lowest health outcomes and literacy rates in the country.

I gravitated toward high-intensity spaces: emergency rooms,

trauma units, critical care. There was something about urgency, the constant demand for clear thinking and quick decisions, which pulled me in. I admired my colleagues, the physicians and nurses who made impossible choices under crushing pressure. However, I also saw the cost it took from them.

My work as a social worker extended beyond just patients. I was there for families, for communities, and often for the care of teams themselves. I was the one they called when a child died, when a woman arrived bruised and broken from an abusive partner. When the "dead on arrival" was the son of the ER physician on duty.

Our way of coping? Camaraderie, inside jokes that only made sense in scrubs, shared exhaustion, and quiet debriefs in supply rooms or parking lots. It was its own kind of therapy, not always clinical, but necessary. Each trauma felt like another emergency code. We responded instinctively, reset emotionally as best we could, and moved on to the next patient, the next shift, the next crisis. We did not pause to process. That was not how the system worked. We stayed in motion because standing still meant feeling too much.

Many experiences from that time led to early awareness of workforce mental health before it was formally recognized. I saw early signs of burnout. I saw compassion fatigue in the eyes of nurses who could not bring themselves to cry. I saw doctors experience moral distress when they had to choose between efficiency and dignity, protocol and compassion.

I also saw what happened when teams had no space to process everything. There was no real infrastructure, no language, and no leadership that knew how to say, *"Let us pause. How are you doing?"*

NAMING THE INVISIBLE WEIGHT

Over the years, I noticed that what we carried home from the hospital was not all the same. Some of us were worn down. Some were running on fumes. Some were living with deeper wounds that no amount of rest could touch. At first, I did not have the words for these differences; they were just things I felt in my gut. Later, I learned there was a language for them.

Understanding the difference between burnout, depletion, moral distress, and moral injury became a turning point for me. It gave shape to the invisible weight we were all carrying, and it helped me see that each required its own kind of healing.

BURNOUT, DEPLETION, MORAL DISTRESS, AND MORAL INJURY – THROUGH A HUMAN LENS

Term	What It Feels Like	Where it Comes From	Common Situations	What Helps You Heal
Burnout	The slow fade-your energy, patience, and sense of purpose get worn down until you are running on autopilot.	The daily grind that never lets up, with little or no space to recover.	Endless shifts, constant changes, and feeling like you cannot catch up.	Lightening the load, clearer roles, leaders who notice and care.
Depletion	The tank is bone dry; even a weekend off does not touch the exhaustion.	Push yourself past the point of emptiness for too long.	Covering shifts for months, skipping real breaks, always "on call".	Proper rest, not just time off; doing things that fill you back up.
Moral Distress	The knot in your stomach when you know what is right but cannot do it.	Barriers that stop you from acting on your values.	I want to give the patient more time, but I am being told to discharge. I am watching a colleague getting mistreated.	Having a voice in decisions, safe places to speak honestly, and bending rules for humanity when you can.
Moral Injury	A deep wound to your sense of who you are and what you stand for.	Experience or being a part of something that goes against core beliefs.	Witnessing neglect, being forced into choices that cause harm, and feeling abandoned by leadership.	Naming the harm, being heard and validated, healing in community, trauma-informed support.

Once I could name these experiences, I began to see them everywhere — in my colleagues, myself, in the systems we worked in. That awareness became the seed for every policy I have written, every program I have built, and every well-being initiative I have led.

I think back to my twenty-something self, a young social worker sitting in a supply closet beside a nurse who had just lost her third pediatric AIDS patient that day. We sat there in the dim light, both of us trying to figure out how to keep doing this work and still hold on to our humanity.

We all had our coping mechanisms. Some moments were quiet and brief: inside jokes at work, quick chats by the wall, or exhausted pauses in the parking lot. It was not formal therapy, but it was what we had. We did not stop long enough to process what had happened. Standing still meant feeling too much, so we stayed in motion.

WHEN DISASTER IS THE JOB

In the 1990s, Tulane University's School of Social Work was ahead of its time. Tulane's curriculum is designed for the Gulf South, focusing on disaster response, environmental hazards, and systemic trauma rather than standard office-based clinical practice.

Our coursework emphasized trauma-informed care and crisis response before those terms were standard. My internship at Charity Hospital in New Orleans, one of the busiest trauma hospitals in the country, was a baptism by fire. It taught me how to keep my voice steady when everything around me was unraveling, how to hold space when the system itself was failing.

That training became the backbone of my career. After Hurricane Katrina, Tulane expanded disaster and resilience education through the School of Social Work and the Disaster Resilience Leadership Academy (DRLA). Later, I would attend Arizona Trauma Institute and become a certified clinical trauma specialist, returning for additional training. Those skills became essential.

Still, even years later, I can close my eyes and see that tiny baby on the gurney. It was the day my professional and personal worlds collided. That moment was my first deep-end plunge, but it would not be my last. What I did not know then was that learning how to name and navigate those invisible wounds would become not just part of my job, but the mission that has shaped my life.

3

HOW WE GOT SO DEPLETED
The Cost of Living in Crisis Mode

You start the day already behind. The unit is short-staffed again. By 7:20 a.m., you are running a code. The house manager calls at 8:05—three admits are waiting in the ER. By 10:00, you have not eaten, four discharges have no rides, and a surprise inspection is circling. Lunchtime brings two deaths and one violent outburst, and you still have not eaten. Your child's school leaves three voicemails you do not answer.

At 4:30, your feet burn, a family needs to talk, and you swallow tears in the hallway. At 7:00 p.m., you get home, realize a granola bar is your only meal, and someone at your kitchen table asks why you are so quiet. None of it is dramatic. All of it is ordinary. That is the problem (Shanafelt & Noseworthy, 2017).

In crisis-tested systems, endurance gets mistaken for strength long after it becomes a warning sign (West et al., 2020). Healthcare trains us to keep moving—one more shift, one more room, one more disaster—until "keep going" becomes a reflex the world expects, and we cannot turn off. The result is not just burnout; It is depletion: body, mind, and spirit run at a deficit for so long that shutdown feels like the only option (Maslach & Leiter, 2016).

Depletion is not an individual failure. It is what happens when organizations live in crisis mode and treat recovery as optional (National Academies of Medicine, 2022).

This chapter makes the case that depletion is physiological, cultural, and operational—and that it hits everyone in the house, from bedside to business office. If we want to keep people, we must redesign the work, not just coach the workers.

HURRICANE KATRINA AND THE LESSON OF CRISIS WITHOUT RECOVERY

Nowhere is the danger of crisis without recovery more evident than in the back-to-back devastation that Louisiana, Mississippi, and Texas faced in 2005. Hurricane Katrina is regarded as one of the most devastating natural disasters in United States history, resulting in the displacement of over one million individuals, more than 1,800 fatalities, and damages exceeding $125 billion (Knabb et al., 2005). The storm also decimated Louisiana's healthcare system. Hospitals across the New Orleans area lost power, flooded, and ran out of supplies (Rudowitz et al., 2006).

Of the sixteen acute-care hospitals in the region, two-thirds closed; only three—Ochsner Health, West Jefferson Medical Center, and East Jefferson Medical Center—remained operational. Among those lost was Charity Hospital of New Orleans, the state's largest teaching hospital with 2,680 beds and the primary training site for thousands of doctors and nurses. Its permanent closure left a void not only in patient care but also in professional education. The storm also displaced 4,500 active physicians from Orleans, Jefferson, and St. Bernard parishes (Rudowitz et al., 2006).

Just one month later, Hurricane Rita struck southwestern Louisiana, compounding the crisis. Hospitals located in southwestern Louisiana and southeast Texas were evacuated or closed because of flooding and power outages. Resources were depleted and trauma compounded in already struggling communities.

Taken together, the two storms severely damaged 60% of

the landmass of Louisiana, either through direct storm surge, flooding, or wind-related destruction (FEMA, 2006; Louisiana Recovery Authority, 2007). Imagine 60% of the state you live in rendered uninhabitable or unsafe within four weeks, homes gone, hospitals shut down, schools closed, neighborhoods scattered. That was the reality for Louisiana.

Though twenty years have passed, many still feel the event occurred recently. The emotional and systemic scars remain. These twin disasters made it clear: resilience in healthcare is not about "bouncing back." It is about building systems capable of enduring what keeps coming. In Louisiana, crisis is not theoretical; it is personal and persistent.

WHEN DISASTER HITS HOME

For me, Hurricane Rita was not just a headline or policy challenge; it was home.

I lived in New Orleans for five years while attending graduate school and working as a medical social worker. However, my roots were deeper in South Louisiana, Acadiana, or as most people call it, Cajun country. My dad worked in the oil field, and I spent much of my childhood in the towns of Cameron and Abbeville.

As Rita barreled toward the coast, I was focused on convincing my family to evacuate two hours north to my home in Baton Rouge. Just weeks after Katrina, our home had already become a refuge—a temporary stop for friends and family from New Orleans, displaced medical students and residents, even reporters covering the crisis. Everyone we knew had opened their doors. It was how we survived.

The night Rita made landfall, twenty-five of us crowded into our living room, watching in stunned silence as the images came in. I will never forget the next morning—seeing Lt. General Russell Honoré, head of the Hurricane Katrina task force, flying over the wreckage with a national news crew. From the helicopter, he said words that broke me: *"The town of Cameron has vanished."*

I burst into tears.

My husband's family is from Lake Charles, just north of Cameron. My dad worked all over that region. We lived there. I knew those streets. Then came more news: my hometown, Abbeville, had flooded. Our childhood home was underwater. My dad called every connection he had, desperate to get back and see it for himself.

A week later, when the roads finally opened, we drove down to witness the damage for ourselves.

I still do not know how to describe what we saw. Trees without leaves, graves and coffins on roadways, dead animals everywhere. The only word that fits is **apocalyptic**.

Driving into Abbeville was like moving through a memory turned to ash. Every house, my aunts', uncles', and cousins', was gutted, broken, or coated in thick brown sludge. When we reached home, I saw my sister standing outside with a broom, tears streaming down her face, sweeping dried mud from what used to be the front walkway. The house behind her was full of people hauling out furniture and ruined belongings. She said she felt powerless to help, so she just started sweeping. It was all she could think of doing.

The memory of my sister sweeping mud outside a ruined house is etched in my mind. Writing about these 20 years later still brings tears to my eyes. A symbol of helplessness, yes, but also of stubborn, aching love for the place we came from.

Disasters are not just headlines when you live in the middle of them. They are your coworkers. Your patients. Your parking lot. Moreover, in health systems across the country, tragedy does not stay on the television — it walks through the hospital doors — the emotional toll is exponential. These are not abstract crises. They are people we know, places we love, and lives we are trying to hold together while still doing our jobs.

THE GENERAL IN THE STORM...

In any major emergency, hospitals activate a central hub known as the command center. Every hospital does it differently, but at ours, the most senior leaders each had clearly defined roles. At the helm was a nursing supervisor who would later become our Chief Nursing Officer, Nicole.

I have never served in the military, but watching Nicole during a crisis was like watching a seasoned field commander, calm, focused, and precise. She managed the chaos with clarity, redirecting resources, solving problems in real time, and keeping communication steady when everything else was falling apart. Those among us with military backgrounds affectionately called her "The General"—and the name stuck.

Typically, a hospital command center runs for a day before a storm and a day or two after. However, after Hurricane Katrina, ours stayed open for weeks. Nicole was still leading when Hurricane Rita came barreling toward the opposite side of the state.

At the time, our hospital was one of the largest in Louisiana. We have become a central transfer hub for patients coming from smaller, overwhelmed hospitals in disaster zones. The pressure was relentless. Nicole carried it all, professionally, expertly, without complaint.

Then came the call that no leader is ever prepared for.

Nicole's father phoned to tell her that her grandmother, who was living in a nursing home, had developed a gastrointestinal bleed. She needed emergency surgery. The hospital was just 1.8 miles away—but no ambulances were available. All resources were tied up in the regionwide disaster response.

Nicole's grandmother died waiting for an ambulance.

Imagine overseeing the coordination of patient transfers across a statewide disaster response—and still being unable to take care of your own family. That is a level of trauma that most people will never understand. However, in healthcare leadership, it happens more often than we talk about.

This is what trauma can look like in systems leadership. Not just exhaustion or tough decisions—but the devastation of knowing that even your best efforts were not enough. Nicole kept leading. She stayed in the command center. However, the weight of that loss was undeniable.

This is why recovery must follow resilience, because even the strongest leaders break when there is no space to grieve.

WHEN THE DISASTERS STACK UP

In 2016, the city of Baton Rouge endured two devastating events that profoundly impacted the emotional fabric of our community. First came the fatal police shooting of Alton Sterling, followed by days of protest, public grief, and national scrutiny. Tensions were high. Just days later, those emotions turned to horror when a sniper ambushed six law enforcement officers, killing three, in a targeted attack.

The loss was personal in a city where first responders form a close-knit community. Many of us in healthcare worked side by side with those officers, some serving on off-duty shifts in our ER. Our nurses and physicians knew them by name. The grief was not abstract; it was visceral and intimate, and it came while we were still reeling from the trauma that preceded it.

Just one month later, a catastrophic, unnamed weather event struck south Louisiana. A flood so widespread it would later be called a "1,000-year flood" that displaced more than 100,000 people (National Weather Service, 2017). Over thirty inches of rain fell in just a few days. The event was not designated as a hurricane, which resulted in limited notice and preparation.

Many of our colleagues lost everything in the flood—homes, cars, and possessions. Yet they kept showing up. Some arrived straight from shelters, still in borrowed clothes. Others finished

12-hour shifts only to spend the night tearing out sheetrock or sleeping on friends' couches. They cared for patients while carrying their own unspoken grief and uncertainty, proving that resilience is not about what you have left, but about what you give when you have nothing left to stand on. These events did not just test our infrastructure; they tested our humanity. Each crisis compounded the next.

For many of us, there was no time to process, no pause to grieve. We deferred our pain through trauma after trauma, and that is what defines depletion. Leaders tried to hold everyone together with town halls and newsletters. Chaplains made rounds with tissues and coffee. However, what we really needed was time. We needed space. We needed someone to say: *"Stop. Sit. You are not okay, and that is okay."*

Of course, no one had that luxury, not in a system that never hits pause, and not in a community already devastated.

CASE STUDY:
LEADING WITH CARE IN THE BATON ROUGE FLOOD

During that flood, my team's job was to track affected employees and coordinate support. We were tired and overwhelmed, and doing our best to manage chaos.

Then Mr. John Finan, our health system CEO, walked into the command center. He did not bring a speech or a checklist. He brought clarity. He asked us one question: *"What is the immediate need for our team members affected? Do they need housing, supplies, childcare, transportation?"* That single question reframed the room. Instead of getting bogged down in reports or policies, the focus turned immediately to people and what would help them most.

That was not just symbolic. At the time, nearly one in five of our system's employees, more than 2,200 people, had lost or severely damaged homes. At Our Lady of the Lake alone, hundreds of staff were working 12–18-hour shifts, sleeping on cots or air mattresses in the hospital. Floodwater surrounded our Livingston emergency department, and supplies had to be flown in by helicopter with the help of the Coast Guard. Patient volumes spiked from an average of 300 to nearly 400 per day, and yet, despite their own losses, team members kept showing up (Catholic Health World, October 2016)

Mr. Finan made sure the organization responded just as quickly as its people. Within 24 hours, affected employees received $1,000 in immediate relief. A fund was launched that grew to half a million dollars. Childcare, clothing, and housing support were organized, and Catholic Charities embedded a case manager to help staff navigate recovery (Catholic Health World, Leadership Profile, 2017). All of that flowed from the same posture of leadership I saw in the command center that day—clear, compassionate, and focused on people first.

That moment still sticks with me. Not due to any resource that was offered, but because it conveyed the statement: *"You matter."* In times of disaster, the most effective leaders are not the ones with the thickest binders or the most extended plans; they are the ones who act decisively and communicate care in real time. That kind of leadership does not erase the damage, but it anchors people in the belief that they are not alone as they begin to recover.

THE YEAR THAT BROKE THE BASELINE

Between 2020 and 2021, Louisiana endured a punishing one-two blow: a relentless string of hurricanes—Laura, Delta, Zeta, and Ida—and the unyielding grip of the COVID pandemic. It was just one blow after another. The storms killed more than **160 people in Louisiana**, caused billions in damage, and left behind weeks-long blackouts and mountains of debris (Louisiana Department of Health, 2022). Coastal towns faced levee breaches and catastrophic flooding, while inland communities like Houma and Thibodaux struggled with mangled infrastructure, uprooted trees, and shuttered businesses.

However, these disasters did not strike in isolation. They collided in real time. The COVID pandemic had already claimed the lives of **over 18,000 Louisianans**, pushed hospitals to the brink, disrupted supply chains, and left thousands grieving loved ones or grappling with job loss (Johns Hopkins University, 2021). Evacuations became a high-stakes calculation—risk crowded shelters and infection or remain in the path of the storm. Recovery was delayed due to fewer workers, safety measures, and limited resources.

The pandemic amplified the hurricanes' devastation, and the hurricanes deepened the pandemic's toll—each feeding the other's impact until the crises were inseparable. What might have been singular, monumental disasters became a compounded humanitarian and economic catastrophe from which Louisiana is still clawing its way back.

Layered trauma. No recovery window. No reset. This was not just a crisis, but a sustained depletion. No one was immune.

SYSTEMS THAT DEMAND MORE WITHOUT GIVING MORE

The hardest part? The system does not slow down when we break.

Hospitals keep operating. Metrics still matter. Leadership meetings are still going on. However, behind the charts and dashboards, people are unraveling.

I have seen staff throw up in bathrooms from anxiety, then go straight back to patient care. I have watched residents fall asleep in rounds. I have heard leaders whisper that they have not had a real day off in years.

Furthermore, I have been that leader. Nodding in meetings and smiling on camera and falling apart in private.

RESEARCH DOES NOT LIE

The data have been telling the same story for years. During COVID, national leaders warned of a "parallel pandemic" of clinician distress that would undermine care if left unaddressed; they called for coordinated, system-level action rather than more individual coping tips (Shanafelt et al., 2020). Large-scale professional surveys of nurses have described astonishing levels of emotional exhaustion and intent to leave, attributing these numbers to staffing, safety, and respect rather than personal resilience (American Nurses Foundation, 2021).

Moral distress—first articulated in the ethics literature as the pain of knowing the right action but being unable to take it—was not a niche concept anymore; it was a daily reality across roles, stacking into what researchers call moral residue that echoes forward and intensifies the next hit.

Together, the evidence is plain: living in crisis mode corrodes judgment, safety, retention, and the bottom line—not because people are weak, but because the system keeps asking for physiologically impossible things and calling it professionalism. Similar patterns appear outside the United States, where national staff surveys report parallel spikes in exhaustion and intent to leave tied to workload, and physical and psychological safety.

WHAT DEPLETION REALLY IS (AND IS NOT)

Burnout says, "I am tired." Depletion says, "I am empty, and no one sees it." Crisis floods the body with cortisol and keeps it there. Sleep breaks. Memory frays. Executive function falters (McEwen, 2004). The amygdala stays hot; the prefrontal cortex keeps dropping out (Arnsten, 2009). This is not a weakness—It is biology.

Minor stressors feel like cliffs because the system cannot downshift. This is not a weakness. It is neurobiology doing what neurobiology does when survival mode never turns off.

It shows up as quiet signals. You stop laughing at jokes you used to love. You forget simple things. You dread work, but you go anyway. You wake up tired and fall asleep exhausted. You cry at the gas pump. Alternatively, you cannot cry at all. It manifests in behavior, including flat affect or overreaction, withdrawal, avoidance of eye contact, and debriefing. It shows up in cognition: lapses, narrowed focus, and catastrophizing. It presents in the body as headaches, chest tightness, and gastrointestinal trouble with no apparent cause. It appears in the soul: numbness, loss of purpose, distance from meaning. None of those points to personal failure. All of them point to a system symptom.

Most of us do not break during the crisis. We break after the adrenaline washes out and the room goes quiet. The pattern repeats: crisis hits, and you perform; immediate recovery comes with praise, and you think you are fine; fatigue creeps in, and the edges sharpen; grief or numbness lands; disillusionment follows, and you think about quitting. Each cycle leaves a residue that makes the next one heavier.

THE HIDDEN WORKFORCE CARRYING THE LOAD

Burnout is not just a bedside problem. Approximately 50% of the workforce in various health systems is classified as non-clinical (Bureau of Labor Statistics, 2023). Their stress rarely makes headlines, but burnout among IT, HR, food service, environmental services, and scheduling shows up as system failures that directly affect patient care (West et al., 2018).

Their pressure is constant and public-facing, but their pain is invisible in the "healthcare heroes" narrative. Understaffed non-clinical teams can slow revenue cycles, increase claim denials, delay security ticket resolution, and reduce the availability of HR support.

Front-desk detachment changes the first five minutes of a patient visit. IT fatigue means slower responses to downtime and longer exposure to risk. These teams experience their own moral distress when they believe in a mission and are unable to fix a broken process that continues to harm people. They move with the same urgency as clinical staff during surges, often without the same recovery resources. If your well-being plan only covers scrubs, you will miss the fuse that keeps blowing.

4

BEYOND THE HOSPITAL WALLS
The Unseen Backbone of Healthcare

FROM ROADSIDE TO BEDSIDE – A SHARED SHIFT

At 6:15 a.m., Maria snaps on gloves in the hallway of Bayou Haven Nursing Home. The air smells faintly of lemon oil and burnt coffee. She starts with Mr. Landry—lift, turn, wash, dress, smile—and moves on to the next call light. By 9:00, she answered twenty. There is no time for breakfast. Her back aches already. Maria is one of the 60% of nursing home staff who report symptoms of burnout, a rate that spiked during the pandemic and has never fully receded (National Academies, 2019; White et al., 2021).

Her exhaustion is not from one bad month or a single crisis. It is the accumulation of years where recovery was never long enough to heal; COVID surges, back-to-back hurricane seasons, ice storms that cut power to oxygen concentrators. Each time, Maria came to work. Each time, she gave the patients what she had left. Each time, recovery was measured in hours, not weeks.

Across town, DeShawn's first EMS call comes at 6:42. An overdose. Then an uncontrolled bleed. Then a welfare check that turns into a septic transport. He knows Bayou Haven well; two of today's calls will take him there. Paramedics like him face burnout rates approaching 50%, with studies linking chronic stress to higher turnover, disrupted sleep, and elevated PTSD risk (Hennein & Lowe, 2020; Halpern et al., 2009).

By 9:10, Maria calls the nurse for a resident whose breathing has worsened. The nurse calls EMS. DeShawn responds with lights and sirens, preparing for oxygen and IV access. Ten minutes later, he is at Maria's side, crouching over the patient. They work as if they have done this together for years—because in a way, they have. Their partnership, shaped by constant emergencies, is implicit.

THE BACKBONE WE KEEP OVERLOOKING

It is easy to picture hospitals when we think of healthcare, but a huge share of essential care happens far from hospital walls. Certified nursing assistants, EMTs, paramedics, home health nurses, hospice aides, and mental health counselors manage most of the responsibility. Alongside them are the non-clinical team: environmental services, dietary, transport, scheduling, security—without whom the entire system would collapse.

Underpaying, understaffing, or failing to recognize work creates systemic fragility within organizations. In places hit by serial disasters, where hurricanes, pandemics, and community violence converge on the same workforce, the risk of attrition accelerates (Brooks et al., 2020). Disaster recovery research confirms what Maria and DeShawn already know: repeated crises shorten coping windows, increase moral injury, and push people out of the field faster (Pfefferbaum & North, 2020; Watson et al., 2011).

Resilience here is not about "bouncing back" after a single blow. It is about designing recovery into the work itself, with the same rigor used to redesign an ICU or surgical service. Without that, every new disaster lands on an already depleted workforce.

WHAT THE DATA ALREADY SHOWS

The evidence reads like a transcript of Maria's and DeShawn's days.

During COVID surges, nursing-home staff reported grief, fear, and moral distress that wellness tips could not touch (White et al., 2021). EMS crews ran COVID-positive calls back-to-back, only to return weeks later for hospice transfers—no recovery in between (National Academies, 2019). After hurricanes, home health aides waded through flooded neighborhoods and downed power lines to reach patients tethered to oxygen.

The findings are sobering:

- High turnover in nursing homes predicts lower quality of care and worsened patient outcomes after disasters.
- EMS burnout after repeated mass-casualty or natural disaster response is associated with elevated PTSD symptoms and a higher likelihood of leaving within three years (Pfefferbaum et al., 2012).
- Chronic understaffing in home health during and after disasters destabilizes continuity of care, raises hospital readmissions, and increases worker injury rates (Gandhi et al., 2021).
- Early well-being screening tools like the Well-Being Index and Impact of Event Scale can detect distress before it escalates into attrition (Shanafelt & Noseworthy, 2017; Watson et al., 2011).

None of these studies names Maria or DeShawn. But every one of them describes their world.

A WORKFORCE ON THE BRINK

Even before COVID, the pipeline of applicants for nursing homes, home health, and EMS were narrowing. Layer repeated hurricanes, pandemic surges, and community violence events, and coping reserves shrink even further (Brooks et al., 2020).

In certain areas, there are three job openings for every applicant. Long-term care facilities report annual turnover up to 60%. EMS agencies see similar turnover, especially among younger medics. The result is a state of perpetual triage—not just for patients, but for the workforce itself.

The challenge is not simply recruitment; It is retention in a reality where demand never lets up. Without targeted interventions, those remaining will be overworked, and more people will depart.

BAYOU HAVEN AND A DAY IN MOTION

Bayou Haven sits behind a stand of live oaks on a two-lane road; the kind of long-term care facility families choose because the lobby smells of lemon oil and the receptionist knows their names. On paper, the staffing grid looks fine. In real life, one sick call turns a normal day into a scramble.

Maria starts with Mr. Landry, a retired welder who jokes in Cajun French and hides butter cookies in his nightstand. Chris, her partner, is new and still learning how to move a grown adult without straining his shoulder. Tessa, the nurse in charge, floats between rooms, answering a daughter's hospice questions while fielding an alert about blood sugar in the forties.

At 9:10, a resident two doors down begins to decline. Jorge, the hospice aide, sits quietly at her bedside, rubbing lotion into her hands. When she dies just before 10, Jorge pulls the sheet up with care and pauses. There is no time to stop: the phone rings, a lift squeals, EVS slips in to clean the room. The team gathers for a three-minute hallway check-in: what happened, who needs a breather, who will call the son.

Across town, DeShawn answers three more calls before noon. Some could have been avoided with more hands in the nursing home. He says it without judgment—just physics. Too few people. Too much to do.

By the time the administrator stops by to talk about a

corrective action plan, his best people are already running on fumes. After work, Maria will reheat leftovers, doze on the couch, and wake to texts about the faulty lift, tomorrow's assignments, and Jorge's quiet message: *"I wish we had had a few minutes for Mrs. B."*

BY THE NUMBERS – BEYOND THE HOSPITAL WALLS

Role	Burnout Rate	Average Pay	Annual Turnover
Nursing Home Staff	~60%	~$17/hour	40–60%
Home Health Aides	~57%	~$16/hour	60–82%
Paramedics / EMTs	~50%	~$23/hour	20–30%

Sources: U.S. Bureau of Labor Statistics (2023); National Academies of Sciences (2019); Templeton et al. (2019); American Ambulance Association Workforce Data (2022).

WHAT COULD CHANGE THE STORY CRISIS-TESTED INTERVENTIONS

Evidence from serial disaster recovery makes it clear: interventions must be predictable, embedded, and repeated after every crisis to work (Watson et al., 2011; Pfefferbaum & North, 2020).

1. **Safe Staffing Ratios & Flexible Scheduling**
   - o Stable staffing improves outcomes and reduces turnover (Aiken et al., 2014).
   - o Post-crisis decompression shifts shorten time to recovery.
2. **Peer Support & Structured Debriefing**
   - o Critical incident stress debriefings within 72 hours reduce cumulative trauma (Mitchell, 2011).
3. **Mental Health Access Without Stigma**
   - o Confidential counseling and leaders modeling

help-seeking increase uptake (Shanafelt & Noseworthy, 2017).

4. **Career Pathways & Recognition**
    - o Skill ladders and pay incentives improve retention, especially when tied to disaster response competencies.
5. **Safety & Equipment Investments**
    - o Reliable lifts, adequate PPE, and vehicle maintenance prevent injury and preserve capacity.
6. **Real-Time Well-Being Monitoring**
    - o Anonymous check-ins detect distress early, allowing targeted intervention.

CLOSING NOTE

Maria, DeShawn, Jorge, and thousands like them are the connective tissue of healthcare. Their work is quiet, often unseen, but essential. I learned this lesson not just in the classroom or through research, but in the days after Katrina and Rita, when nursing assistants, EMTs, and home health workers kept showing up even as their own homes were flooded, their families displaced, and their futures uncertain.

Back then, I saw with my own eyes how the people we so often overlook became the ones holding fragile systems together. Today, the same story continues. If we keep asking them to endure without building recovery into the very structure of their work, we will lose them—and with them, the fragile stability of our entire system.

5

BEYOND BURNOUT
What Healthcare Can No Longer Ignore

The overhead lights are too bright for 5:47 a.m., but the hospital does not keep sunrise hours. The day's first code has been called. In the emergency room, the night shift finishes charting at the same speed they use to hang fluids. The day shift stands at the edge of the nurses' station, scanning assignment boards like weather maps—checking for where the storms will be.

In one corner, a respiratory therapist rubs her temples, trying to remember the last day she did not dream about alarms. Down the hall, a tech hums a tune while cleaning a room, the same song she has used to fill the silence for years. A physician flips through a mental checklist, skipping breakfast because there is no time and no appetite.

None of them looks "in crisis." No one is crying. However, all of them are carrying the weight of years—pandemics, hurricanes, mass shootings, systematic strain—stacked without space to recover. In healthcare, disasters rarely arrive one at a time anymore. They layer. They overlap. They compound.

This is **cumulative strain in a serial disaster environment**. It is not a single dramatic breaking point. Prolonged exposure to stress may lead to burnout, and in some instances, can result in trauma or moral injury. The challenge lies in the fact that the tipping point cannot be identified until it has already been surpassed.

THE STRESS → BURNOUT → TRAUMA CONTINUUM IN SERIAL DISASTERS

Stress is the body's push to meet a challenge. In short bursts, it can sharpen focus and improve performance. However, in serial disasters, stress is not short-term. The pace remains consistent, the level of importance is elevated, and opportunities for recovery are limited. The emotional aftershocks of one event collide with the onset of the next.

Burnout develops when that constant stress hardens into a chronic state—function continues, but the spark is gone. You feel flat, detached, and ineffective. Trauma goes further. The world is changing. Your nervous system stays in survival mode, shaped by **repeated exposure** rather than one isolated crisis (Morganstein & Ursano, 2020). PTO and a meditation app cannot undo it.

Disaster mental health research emphasizes that in high-exposure professions, recovery must be **tiered and sustained**—stepped care that addresses acute symptoms, builds social connection, and follows through for months after the last headline (SAMHSA, 2014; NASEM, 2019).

Many clinicians experience what psychologist Corey Keyes describes as **languishing**. Not in crisis, not well. They show up, chart, and round, but the light is out behind their eyes. In serial disaster recovery literature, this is the danger zone: one stressor away from collapse.

WHAT EVIDENCE TELLS US

The research aligns with what disaster-tested teams already know:

- **Pandemic-era long-term care studies** documented grief, fear, and exhaustion that quick wellness tips could not touch—**sustained depletion** from overlapping crises. (White et al., 2021).

- **Turnover analyses** in disaster contexts show instability is both a **symptom and a driver** of diminished care quality. The cost of replacing healthcare staff—already high—rises sharply when communities are simultaneously recovering from disasters (Han et al., 2019).
- **Behavioral health integration models** from the disaster literature show that early screening with tools like the Mayo Clinic Well-Being Index, paired with stepped-care referrals, can reduce downstream burnout and PTSD (Shanafelt & Noseworthy, 2017; SAMHSA, 2014).

Healthcare systems that regard recovery as a fundamental component of their infrastructure, rather than an optional addition, tend to achieve higher retention rates, improve recovery timelines, and enhance preparedness for future crises.

WHY WE BREAK DIFFERENTLY

Not everyone's path through the stress-to-trauma continuum looks the same. Adverse childhood events, past trauma, gender, and coping style shape responses. In disaster behavioral health, risk and resilience factors help identify individuals who may require extended support.

Nurses, physicians, paramedics, and advanced practice clinicians carry overlapping burdens and distinct ones. Nurses shoulder relentless physical work and emotional proximity: lifting bodies, twelve-hour shifts, eyes on families in every stage from admission to death. They are often protocol-bound in understaffed rooms where their voice does not carry far enough, which compounds fatigue with invisibility.

Physicians face a different pressure point: decision fatigue under liability, eroding autonomy as payers and dashboards shape practice, and a slow severing from the reasons they entered the field. Some rush to escape emotion. Others go silent. A physician assistant once told me:

"We did not cry in my house. Emotions were weak. So, when patients die, I speed up. I do not process until I am home. Sometimes I do not process at all."

Recovery timelines are not linear. In serial disasters, the "next event" can interrupt healing from the last—leaders who design supports for a mythical "average employee" risk **leaving the most vulnerable unprotected**.

THE DEEP CUT OF MORAL DISTRESS IN DISASTER CONTEXTS

Moral distress, first described by Andrew Jameton in 1984, is the pain of knowing the right course but being unable to act because of constraints. In serial disasters, these constraints multiply: rationing ICU beds during a pandemic, discharging patients into unsafe homes after a hurricane, delaying care because of supply shortages.

When unresolved, these moments leave **moral residue** that stacks with each disaster, creating what Epstein & Hamric call the **crescendo effect**. Left unaddressed, moral injury erodes trust, fractures teams, and drives people entirely from the profession.

TRAUMA-INFORMED LEADERSHIP AS A SERIAL DISASTER RECOVERY STRATEGY

Depletion in serial disaster contexts rarely shouts. It hides under professionalism, perfectionism, and over-functioning. The signs are often subtle: frequent lateness that signals exhaustion or overwhelm; irritability that reflects emotional fatigue; disengagement that points to burnout or hopelessness. Even over-functioning—the "rocks" everyone leans on—can mask avoidance of pain. The hardest to spot are those we depend on most, until they can no longer carry the weight.

Recognizing these quiet indicators is only the first step. Awareness without action risks leaving suffering unaddressed. Once we see the patterns of depletion and distress, the question becomes: how do leaders respond? Correcting performance or offering surface-level wellness programming may miss the underlying injury. A framework is needed that recognizes how repeated stress and trauma can influence behavior, performance, and health.

If burnout is the warning light and trauma is the engine damage, trauma-informed leadership is the mechanic who lifts the hood before the engine seizes. It is not a wellness trend but a recovery strategy.

WHY IT MATTERS IN SERIAL DISASTERS:

- Healthcare workplaces are high-exposure environments where acute and cumulative trauma are both part of the job description (Green et al., 2021).
- Trauma changes cognition, communication, and self-regulation—leaders who miss these shifts risk misreading their staff as "difficult" rather than "distressed" (SAMHSA, 2014).
- Leadership style can compound harm or promote recovery. Disaster recovery studies emphasize transparent, flexible, and supportive leadership as critical to retention and morale (O'Donovan & McAuliffe, 2020).

This perspective sets the stage for concrete practices—core principles of trauma-informed leadership that can be adapted for disaster recovery contexts.

CORE PRINCIPLES IN DISASTER-ADAPTED TRAUMA-INFORMED LEADERSHIP

(Adapted from SAMHSA's Six Principles, Harris & Fallot, and healthcare disaster recovery literature)

1. **Safety**
   - **Physical: Safe staffing levels, PPE, hazard mitigation (West et al., 2018).**
   - **Psychological: Post-incident decompression time before returning to high-acuity work.**
2. **Trustworthiness & Transparency**
   - **Real-time explanations for operational changes during disasters (SAMHSA, 2014).**
3. **Peer Support**
   - **Structured peer debriefs like the Resilience and Coping for the Healthcare Community (RCHC) model post-disaster (Yuma et al., 2019).**
4. **Collaboration & Mutuality**
   - **Flattened hierarchy in problem-solving—engage all disciplines in disaster planning.**
5. **Empowerment & Choice**
   - **Flexible scheduling and voluntary opt-out from high-trauma assignments post-crisis.**
6. **Cultural, Historical, & Gender Awareness**
   - **Disaster impacts vary by culture, history, and gender, so responses should consider these factors.**

LEADER PRACTICES FOR SERIAL DISASTER RECOVERY

Observed Pattern	Leader Response
Over-functioning "rocks"	Schedule decompression time within 2 weeks of significant exposure; rotate to lower-acuity duties.
Silent withdrawers	Specific private check-ins offer reassignment; facilitate direct behavioral health contact.
Hyper-aroused responders	Allow micro-pauses; adjust assignments next shift; follow with a one-week touchpoint.
Whole-team strain	Drop low-value tasks; run grief huddles; communicate cause and effect.
Inequitable load	Provide targeted support (childcare stipends, differential pay, tele-debriefs).

THE ORGANIZATIONAL PAYOFF

Evidence from disaster recovery and trauma-informed care shows:

- **Lower turnover** and reduced recruitment costs (Han et al., 2019).
- **Improved patient safety** and quality (Greenberg et al., 2020).
- **Greater team cohesion** (Edmondson, 1999; O'Donovan & McAuliffe, 2020).
- **Reduced presenteeism** and absenteeism (West et al., 2018).

When done well, trauma-informed leadership shifts the culture from **reactive crisis management** to **proactive resilience building**—essential in an era when disasters no longer arrive one at a time.

6

WHY RECOVERY MUST FOLLOW RESILIENCE
Building Sustainable Systems in Healthcare

The generators are still humming when the sun comes up. Night staff passes report with hollow eyes. Someone jokes about coffee, then stares at the wall. The unit is open, patients are alive, and the team is "resilient" by every public measure. Forty-eight hours later, the halls are quiet again, but the damage rides home in the bodies of the people who kept the doors open.

We often mistake endurance for resilience. We celebrate getting through the surge, the storm, the shooting. But resilience without recovery is a strain that eventually snaps (West et al., 2018; National Academy of Medicine [NAM], 2022). The shift this chapter argues for is simple and non-negotiable: build planned, protected recovery into operations the same way you plan surge capacity. Recovery is not a reward or an EAP flyer—it is the only way resilience lasts.

RETHINKING RESILIENCE: A PERSONAL SHIFT

Rethinking resilience required me to ask more complex questions of myself as a leader. It was no longer enough to admire the grit of those who kept showing up day after day. I had to wrestle with the truth that resilience without recovery was unsustainable—and that leadership had a responsibility in shaping the conditions for both.

Reflecting on my leadership journey, I see that early mentors taught me the true meaning of responsibility. At 25, I accepted the role of Director of Medical Social Work, a responsibility that felt both daunting and defining. The decade I spent at General Health System became my training ground for leadership, shaping my voice, refining my values, and clarifying my vision for how leaders create lasting impact.

Tom Sawyer, who served as system CEO for General Health System, carried himself with vision and purpose. He reminded us that healthcare was bigger than any one hospital, it was about building strong institutions, developing future caregivers, and strengthening the communities we served. His passion for medical education and leadership development left a lasting mark on me. Tom Sawyer believed that investing in people was the most important investment of all, and I felt that conviction every time he encouraged growth, challenged us to think bigger, and modeled what it meant to lead with integrity.

At the same time, **Jim Brexler** was shaping the culture within Baton Rouge General Medical Center. His leadership was steady, collaborative, and deeply respectful of staff. He prioritized performance and quality while also considering the impact on individuals. He demonstrated a commitment to building a just culture, one that valued every individual's input and aimed to balance accountability with fairness. Under Jim's guidance, I participated in one of the most impactful leadership development programs I have ever known, an experience that built my confidence and helped me find my footing as a young leader.

It was also during this formative decade that I came under the influence of **Dr. Floyd "Flip" Roberts** and **Dr. Richard "Rick" Streiffer**—two physician leaders who modeled different but equally powerful styles of leadership. From Dr. Roberts, I learned what it meant to be an *academic partnership catalyst.* He had a unique gift for bridging worlds—linking hospitals, universities, and professional organizations in the pursuit of safer, better care. From Rick, I absorbed the importance of being a *builder and innovator.* He created programs, residencies, and departments where none had existed before, proving that leaders must not only sustain what they inherit but also imagine what does not yet exist.

Together, these leaders marked developmental milestones in my journey. They showed me that leadership is not about titles or authority, but about investing in people, building trust, and creating space for others to thrive. Most importantly, they taught me that leadership has a direct impact on well-being. **Three decades later, I continue to carry forward the lessons they taught, investing in people, lifting unheard voices, and making recovery as essential as performance.** Their examples laid the foundation for the work I do today, leading with the conviction that safeguarding the workforce is not a luxury but a necessity for a system's survival.

A WORD ABOUT "TEACHING RESILIENCE"

Every time I hear a national leader say, "We need to teach resilience to our team members," I want to throw up—or throw something across the room. Healthcare workers are some of the most resilient people I know, often exhibiting resilience in their professional roles. It looks like medical students grinding through sleepless rotations. It looks like nurses graduating after years of twelve-hour clinicals while juggling families and night shifts. It looks like EMTs dragging themselves back to the ambulance after coding a child.

That is why knowing your audience matters when you talk about resilience. For young staff just entering healthcare, the concept may be new and helpful. But for those who have carried decades of night shifts, disasters, pandemics, and personal sacrifice, hearing "you just need to be more resilient" stings. It comes across not as wisdom, but as dismissal of the extraordinary resilience they already show every single day.

Furthermore, if you are from the South, you know that *"misinformed"* is just a polite way of saying, ***bless his heart.*** They know not what they say. What these leaders miss is that resilience has never been our gap. Recovery has. If you keep demanding resilience without protecting recovery, you do not get stronger teams, you get broken ones.

WHAT EVIDENCE SHOWS

Research consistently demonstrates that system-level interventions outperform individual-focused "coping skills" programs in reducing burnout and sustaining engagement (West et al., 2020; Panagioti et al., 2017).

Key findings from the literature include:

- Staffing and scheduling adjustments lead to greater reductions in burnout than wellness education alone (West et al., 2018).
- Routine well-being measurement using validated tools (e.g., Mayo Clinic Well-Being Index) can identify distress early and correlate it with turnover risk (Shanafelt et al., 2016).
- Leadership engagement is a primary driver of workforce well-being. The NAM's National Plan calls for leadership accountability, operational barrier removal, and integrated mental health access—not as add-ons, but as embedded processes (NAM, 2022).

When recovery processes are organized and provided with adequate resources, there is an increase in retention and consistent quality outcomes. Where it is optional or "after hours," participation declines and impact fades.

LEADER MOVES THAT MAKE RECOVERY REAL

1. Put Recovery on the Schedule—and Pay for It

Evidence: Paid decompression time following traumatic events reduces PTSD symptoms and improves retention (Bennett et al., 2020).

- Block at least four protected hours within two weeks of sentinel events for those directly involved.
- Cover it on the clock; staff coverage the same way you cover lunch breaks or trauma alerts.
- Fund by pausing low-value projects for a quarter.

2. Give Grief a Place to Go

Evidence: Structured post-event debriefs improve team cohesion and emotional recovery (Teshome et al., 2020).

- Ten minutes after a death or high-stress case: name what happened, surface immediate safety fixes, point to help, acknowledge the work.
- Include all involved disciplines—EVS, dietary, transport—as they carry the event too.

3. Treat Ratios as Harm Reduction

Evidence: Chronic understaffing is strongly associated with burnout, moral distress, and turnover (Ball et al., 2018).

- Stabilize one unit at a time; collapse nonessential services temporarily to redistribute staff.
- Track safety and quality metrics before and after to build a business case.

4. Equip Supervisors to Lead Humans, Not Just Shifts

Evidence: Frontline leaders influence engagement and burnout more than any other organizational factor (Shanafelt &

Noseworthy, 2017).

- Train for spotting distress, defusing conflict, running grief huddles, and starting shifts with, "What do you need to do good work today?"
- Tie evaluations to team well-being alongside budget and audits.

5. **Measure, Close the Loop, and Communicate Change**

Evidence: Transparent feedback loops increase trust and engagement (Bodenheimer & Sinsky, 2014).

- Run monthly pulse surveys for three months post-event.
- Share "We heard → We did → We're still working on" updates.

USE THE NATIONAL PLAN AS THE SPINE

The **National Plan for Health Workforce Well-Being** (NAM, 2022) identifies seven priority areas, all of which can be operationalized into daily leadership:

1. **Leadership commitment**: Model and resource recovery.
2. **Measurement and accountability**: Track well-being as rigorously as safety and finance.
3. **Normalize mental health**: Make support services accessible and stigma-free, integrated into shifts.
4. **Remove workflow drag**: Eliminate low-value tasks and administrative burden.
5. **Make technology humane**: Invest in tools that simplify, not complicate.

6. **Support long-term careers**: Transparent pay, clear advancement, protected professional development.
7. **Build belonging**: Commit to diversity, equity, inclusion, and psychological safety.

FROM AFTERTHOUGHT TO IMPERATIVE

To move beyond token gestures:

- Make well-being an **operational expectation**, not an optional benefit.
- Treat it as a **strategic driver** of quality, retention, and safety.
- Hold **leaders at every level accountable** for culture, not just metrics.
- Tailor interventions to the **cultural and local context** to reduce stigma and increase uptake.

WHAT TO WATCH OUT FOR

Recovery costs time and coverage. Grief huddles cost minutes you think you do not have. Supervisor training pulls leaders off the floor. The trap is trying to do everything lightly and moving nothing. Research indicates that concentrating on selected interventions, providing them with adequate resources, and expanding them following demonstrated effectiveness is a recommended approach (Panagioti et al., 2017).

A DIFFERENT FINISH LINE

Resilience keeps the doors open. Recovery keeps people whole. Without both, we burn through the very workforce we depend on. Structured, protected recovery—scheduled, budgeted, and culturally normalized—turns resilience from a one-time feat into a sustainable capacity.

We cannot stop every crisis, but we can change how it lands. Sustainable systems pair surge planning with recovery planning, protecting judgment, compassion, and operational stability for the long haul.

7

THE SILENCE BEHIND THE SCRUBS
Why We Do Not Ask for Help

Dana was a skilled trauma nurse who had worked every hurricane the Gulf Coast could throw at her. She was a steady, unflappable colleague whom I leaned on when the overhead system announced a trauma alert. After the most recent storm, she worked four back-to-back twelve-hour shifts, sleeping in a call room while her own home sat dark and water-damaged.

Following the restoration of power and the stabilization of patient conditions, the hospital resumed standard operations within days. No decompression. No schedule relief. Dana did not complain, at least not aloud. Three weeks later, she quietly applied for a travel nurse position out of state. The loss was invisible in the spreadsheets, but it was a direct cost of a culture that rewards endurance while ignoring recovery.

Dana's story is not rare. Neglecting well-being can make seeking help risky.

If Chapter 6 showed how strain lands differently, this chapter shows why people still do not ask for help—and what leaders must change so they can.

WHY WE DO NOT ASK FOR HELP

The reasons are as complex as those wearing badges.

1. **Stigma still runs deep.**

In 2025, mental health is still discussed quietly and with care in healthcare settings. These are matters frequently approached with great care. Our organizational culture has evolved to associate strength with discretion in communication. For physicians, residents, and executives, admitting distress can feel like professional self-sabotage.

A 2020 survey by Shanafelt et al. found that 40% of physicians avoided seeking mental health care due to concerns about licensure and professional standing (Shanafelt et al., 2020). I have heard senior leaders say, *"We need our people to be tough,"* while privately confessing they are barely holding it together. In close-knit communities, admitting struggles can feel like disappointing others.

2. Resilience has been mischaracterized.

Resilience training was long seen as the solution to burnout. The intent was good, but the delivery often missed the mark. Too often, "resilience" is misused to mean pushing harder and refusing to break. That is not resilience; it is sustained denial in a clean uniform.

True resilience is about recovery, boundary-setting, and the courage to say, *"I am not okay,"* without fear of losing your place at the table. The National Academies of Sciences, Engineering, and Medicine (2022) explicitly warns against framing resilience as individual grit alone; system-level supports are critical to sustaining workforce well-being. However, instead of that message, too many still hear, *"Be grateful you have a job." "Others have it worse." "You are strong—just keep going."*

3. Fear of consequences.

In smaller healthcare facilities, seeking assistance is frequently perceived as a potential risk. I have spoken to clinicians who avoided in-house counseling because they feared their colleagues would find out. Others worried that a diagnosis in their record might affect licensure, credentialing, or future job prospects.

Empirical research supports these concerns. Dyrbye et al. (2017) found that medical licensure applications in multiple

U.S. states still included questions about past mental health diagnoses, creating a deterrent effect that discourages help-seeking (Mayo Clin Proc, 2017). Until policies shift to focus on *current impairment* rather than any past struggle, silence will remain the safer option.

The privacy piece is genuine. Clinicians avoid in-house counseling due to concerns about confidentiality and potential licensing or credentialing issues. In interviews, people say it plainly: "I cannot risk this getting back to a supervisor," or "I do not know what that question on the renewal form means."

Organizations that fix the policy language by asking about current impairment rather than any past diagnosis, and that provide off-network access with clear firewalls, see higher uptake. Work with legal, compliance, and your medical staff office to align language with your board of trustees' guidance. The goal is clarity that protects patient safety and clinician privacy at the same time.

4. We have normalized suffering.

Healthcare has conditioned its workforce to accept self-sacrifice as the price of admission. We skip meals, miss family milestones, and "just push through" after disasters. After hurricanes, pandemics, or mass casualty events, that mindset only intensifies.

Research from West et al. (2018) finds that chronic overwork leads to burnout, which increases turnover and lowers patient safety and clinical outcomes. Over time, this conditioning dulls awareness of personal limits. Residents have told me they did not realize how bad it was until they could not get out of bed. Leaders admit they have not slept through the night in years

5. Cultural and generational pressures.

For women, professionals of color, and those from underrepresented backgrounds, the unspoken mandate to *prove you belong* adds extra weight. In competitive settings, seeking help may seem like admitting you are unprepared for your current position.

Templeton et al. (2019) found that women physicians experience higher burnout rates than men, often due to disproportionate caregiving burdens and persistent gender bias. For physicians of color, O'Connor et al. (2022) found that systemic racism and microaggressions significantly increase stress load.

Generational differences compound the gap. Younger clinicians may be more willing to discuss mental health, but older leaders—socialized in a "never let them see you sweat" culture—sometimes dismiss them as "soft," reinforcing the silence that drives attrition.

The throughline is this: when the system rewards endurance, misrepresents resilience, punishes honesty, and layers identity-based pressures on top, silence wins. Furthermore, silence, in healthcare, is never neutral; it costs people, patients, and the future of the workforce.

Healthcare trains us to move, not feel. We learn to function under fire, to hold our faces still, to push past the moment so the work can go on. That training saves lives, but it also teaches silence. We do not ask for help because the culture still treats needing it as a personal problem, a privacy risk, a career hazard, or a test of toughness we are supposed to pass alone.

The result is predictable: people perform while they fracture. Silence is not resilience. To keep employees, leaders should make asking for help a regular, supported part of workplace culture. Not a perk after hours. A standard of care inside the workday.

WHAT LEADERS CAN DO NOW (MOVES THAT CHANGE THE ROOM)

These moves fit the framework from Chapter 3 and focus on privacy, stigma reduction, and policies, so help is not just available, it is safe to use and clearly endorsed.

Make help normal at the top.
People copy what the leader models. Name your own limits, share a short recovery story in team settings, and treat well-being check-ins with the same seriousness as performance conversations. Research indicates leaders who show vulnerability are ~60% more likely to foster trust, and their teams show up to ~40% higher resilience with lower turnover (Edmondson, 1999; O'Donovan & McAuliffe, 2020).

Fix the policies that punish candor.
If your forms still ask about lifetime mental-health history, rewrite them to ask only about current impairment. Provide a clear explanation of the purpose for information collection, the methods of data storage, and the individuals or groups granted access (AMA, 2021). Pair that clarity with confidential, off-network counseling that staff can book without a badge trail.

Hard-wire recovery into the schedule.
Decompression cannot depend on favors. After high-impact events—pediatric deaths, mass-casualty responses—put a paid recovery block on the schedule within two weeks. When possible, rotate people from high-stress assignments to lower-acuity work for a short window so the nervous system can reset.

Build a grief practice that fits inside a shift.
Run brief, peer-led huddles after traumatic cases: say what happened, note immediate safety fixes, point to support, then return to care. This is not therapy; it is emotional hygiene. Evidence shows that daily huddles improve communication, safety, and engagement (BioMed Central; PSNet). Back this up with a monthly reflective forum (e.g., Schwartz Rounds) and a quiet friend check-in within 48 hours.

Give privacy and voice real weight in design.
Use short, validated check-ins after critical events to spot distress early. Close the loop in public with simple "We heard → we did" updates—visible to nights and weekends—showing small, concrete changes (retiring low-value tasks, adjusting parking security, smoothing coverage). Track whether use of confidential supports rises as trust grows.

That is, it: model it, protect it in policy, put it on the calendar, make room for grief, and prove—every week—that staff voices change the work.

SPECIAL CONSIDERATIONS: THE WEIGHT WE OFTEN IGNORE

Not all clinicians access help from the same starting point. Women, professionals of color, early-career, and rural staff may carry greater expectations and limited resources.

Action: Compensate for disparities with meaningful support such as childcare stipends, night-shift differentials, tele-debriefing sessions, and initiative-taking mentorship programs.

8

MEASURING THE DAMAGE
How We Know What We Are Facing

The morning safety huddle ends at 7:58 a.m. The unit is already behind. On the whiteboard, someone has drawn a smiley face next to *"Great job, night shift!"* A charge nurse rubs her eyes and circles two initials on the staffing grid. The nurse manager calls at 8:03 to ask if anyone can pick up twelve more hours. At 8:12, a family posts a one-star review about *"cold care."* By 8:15, three people have said the day *"feels rough."*

None of that is structured data—it is an early signal. Two near-miss reports and four sick calls hit the dashboard by 8:25. That is data. The difference matters.

If you want to heal a system, you must measure the injury. Guesswork will not cut it. **Treating burnout and depletion without data is like treating sepsis without lab work; you cannot heal what you have not measured.** Real assessment gives you both a map and permission to act. It shows where distress lives, which levers to pull first, and whether your fixes are working (National Academy of Medicine, 2022).

In single crises, well-being data might dip and then rebound over weeks or months. In situations involving consecutive crises—where a new event occurs before recovery from the previous one—the resulting patterns exhibit distinct characteristics. Slopes flatten, rebound stall, and cumulative injury hides in plain sight unless leaders measure it directly.

This chapter lays out a practical way to measure well-being at two levels—the individual and the organization—and in a way that people trust. We will look at what the evidence shows, how one hospital made measurement part of the workday, the leadership moves that change behavior, and the traps that make measurement useless or harmful.

WHAT EVIDENCE SHOWS

Most validated tools target standard recovery cycles. That does not mean they are useless in serial disasters; it means leaders must interpret them differently. A flat line after a hurricane or mass casualty event does not mean resilience. It may mean exhaustion so profound that staff have no energy left to answer. In back-to-back crises, silence is a signal.

Physician burnout spiked during the pandemic, 63% in 2021, then eased but remained high. By 2023, about 45% of physicians still reported at least one symptom (Shanafelt et al., 2022). That is better than the peak, but still a serious risk pool.

National estimates put the annual cost of physician burnout in billions of dollars through turnover and reduced clinical hours. Localized, that is, a measurable per-physician drag on budget and capacity. Measurement is not a nicety. It is how you protect the balance sheet by protecting the people who keep it in the black.

Nursing tells a parallel story. National RN turnover decreased in 2024 but remained high at 16.4%, with an average hospital losing $4.75 million annually to RN turnover alone. Replacing one bedside nurse runs about $61,000; each single-point change in RN turnover can swing $289,000 for a typical hospital (NSI Nursing Solutions, 2024). Those are not abstract figures; they are budget lines tied to staffing, safety, and outcomes.

Measurement takes time. The cost is insignificant compared

to the unmeasured injury costs. Each nurse you keep saves five figures on replacement costs and, often, six figures if you can reduce travel expenses. The RN turnover data is public and blunt about how a single percentage point moves dollars. If you want CFO support for decompression time, safer assignments after heavy hits, or external counseling access, show how a two-point retention improvement pays for those moves—and then prove it on one unit.

Burnout is not just a morale problem—it is a safety problem. A meta-analysis of forty-seven studies found physician burnout was associated with double the odds of unsafe care and unprofessional behavior (Panagioti et al., 2018). Nurse burnout tracks with lower quality, lower safety, and lower patient satisfaction across settings (Dyrbye et al., 2020). If you care about harm and HCAHPS, you must measure distress with the same discipline you bring to CLABSI or LOS.

You do not need to invent instruments. The **Maslach Burnout Inventory (MBI)** is the research standard for depth (Maslach & Jackson, 1981; Maslach et al., 2018). The **Stanford Professional Fulfillment Index (PFI)** adds a positive lens and is short enough to repeat (Trockel et al., 2018). The **Mayo Clinic Well-Being Index (WBI)** is a brief monthly risk screen that many systems use at scale (Dyrbye et al., 2014). The point is not to collect pretty numbers. The point is to catch risk early, route support fast, and track whether changes help.

National guidance aligns. The ACGME embedded well-being into training requirements years ago (ACGME, 2023). The **National Plan for Health Workforce Well-Being** calls on organizations to measure, de-identify, and use results for internal improvement—not punishment (NAM, 2022). This is not fringe. It is baseline governance.

You will see fewer sick calls, more targeted fixes, earlier hazard detection, and a board conversation that treats well-being as an operational imperative. The literature backs this: well-being measurement, when tied to actionable changes, improves retention, reduces errors, and protects financial performance (Shanafelt et al., 2022; NAM, 2022).

Turning measurement into an operational priority is one thing; seeing it work in practice is another. During my tenure as Chief Academic Officer at Our Lady of the Lake Health, our team saw firsthand that when well-being data is gathered with intention, championed by trusted leaders, and tied to fundamental changes, the impact is measurable. That is why our participation in the Alliance of Independent Academic Medical Centers (AIAMC) National Initiative on physician well-being became a turning point. The AIAMC leads multi-institutional collaboratives that unite academic health systems around pressing issues in healthcare, and in this effort, we joined 34 other hospital systems nationwide to address physician well-being in a coordinated and measurable way.

SURVEYING THE SYSTEM LESSONS FROM THE AIAMC NATIONAL INITIATIVE

Through our participation in the AIAMC (Alliance of Independent Academic Medical Centers) National Initiative on physician well-being, we set out to move beyond assumptions and capture a clear picture of what our physicians and residents were experiencing. To do this, we launched a comprehensive survey using the Maslach Burnout Inventory (MBI), a validated tool widely regarded as the benchmark for assessing emotional exhaustion, depersonalization, and professional fulfillment.

Historically, physician response rates to surveys have been low, leaving leaders with incomplete or unrepresentative data. To overcome this, we deliberately engaged physician leaders as champions—our Chief Medical Officer, the President of our physician group, and the Medical Director of Graduate Medical

Education. Each residency program also appointed a resident champion to ensure peer participation. With this leadership in place, we achieved a 60% response rate, the highest we had ever seen for any initiative of this kind.

The results were revealing: 45% of respondents reported experiencing burnout. Equally important, the drivers varied significantly across groups. Older physicians struggled with adapting to the electronic medical record and the growing regulatory demands. Younger physicians reported feelings of professional isolation. Residents mentioned long work hours and not enough rest.

However, the numbers told only part of the story. To better understand the human reality behind the data, 130 practicing physicians and residents participated in a series of listening sessions, all held over one week and facilitated by an external consultant. These sessions fostered space for candid reflection and revealed what the survey alone could not capture: the challenge was not simply burnout. What surfaced most clearly was depletion—a profound emptiness beyond fatigue—and moral distress, the pain of knowing the right course of action but being unable to pursue it. These deeper wounds demanded responses that went beyond surface-level fixes.

This work unfolded just as the Accreditation Council for Graduate Medical Education (ACGME) introduced formal requirements for faculty and resident well-being. Fortunately, our residency programs were already ahead of the curve in building a culture of support. The survey provided baseline burnout data for each program, establishing a level of transparency that had not existed before. That transparency, combined with the listening sessions, created the foundation for targeted interventions and cultural change. A project turned into a chance to redefine how well-being is measured and addressed.

In response, we hosted a one-day visioning workshop that invited physicians to co-create a picture of what well-being in our organization should look like. This session became a turning point, shifting the conversation from identifying problems to designing solutions.

The visioning session produced a clear set of physician-driven priorities, many of which were immediately translated into action. These initiatives reflected what physicians themselves said would make well-being visible and tangible in their daily work:

1. **Creation of a Joy in Medicine Task Forc**e led by a respected surgeon, Dr. Kelly Finan, to champion well-being efforts.

2. **Designation of EHR champions** to support colleagues struggling with documentation and system inefficiencies.

3. **A retreat for women physicians,** led by Dr. Gigi Dunn, to foster connection, renewal, and peer support.

4. **Social events for physicians and their families,** including tailgates during football season and a popular annual spring crawfish boil (this was Louisiana, after all), that provided opportunities to reconnect outside of work.

5. **Resident appreciation initiatives,** such as Resident Appreciation Week and a Resident of the Month program with names highlighted on hospital-wide boards.

6. **Expansion of wellness curriculum in our residency programs**, including an annual wellness retreat, class-specific team-building retreats, and community outreach.

7. **Creative reflection projects for residents,** such as the Our Lady of the Lake Pediatric Residency Program's *Art in Medicine* initiative, led by Dr. Emily Klepper. This program invites residents to explore the "little things" in medicine through collaborative art, fostering emotional processing and a deeper connection to their calling in medicine.

8. **Launch of a Physician Leadership Academy** to strengthen professional growth, advocacy, and physician voice in organizational decision-making.

These actions did not come from leadership alone; they came directly from listening to physicians and residents. That distinction mattered. It built trust, showed responsiveness, and turned data into transformation. What began as a survey evolved into a movement—embedding well-being as part of the organization's operating culture rather than as a supplemental program.

FROM TALK TO INFRASTRUCTURE

Healthcare will not heal through wellness posters in breakrooms. It will not happen through pizza parties after trauma, or resilience training that suggests burnout is a personal failure.

If we want to build something better, we must reimagine what care looks like — not just for patients, but for providers.

That means asking better questions:

- What if well-being were not a side initiative, but a core metric of organizational health?
- How might outcomes differ if psychological safety receives the same diligence as patient safety?
- What if healthcare leaders learned emotional intelligence and trauma-informed management, not only finance or operations?

Real change does not happen from slogans. It happens from structures. You must build the capacity for emotional recovery the same way you build ICU capacity, proactively, with data, funding, leadership, and a long-range plan.

That shift is not just theoretical. It is happening in certain areas.

HOW TO MEASURE INDIVIDUAL

Not everyone will raise a hand in public. Confidential self-assessment catches distress before it erupts as absence, error, or resignation. Use brief, validated tools:

- **Well-Being Index (WBI):** a two-minute monthly risk screen with published validation (Dyrbye et al., 2014). Built for repetition and routing support.
- **Professional Fulfillment Index (PFI):** short, measures both distress and meaning—protective factors matter (Trockel et al., 2018).
- **Maslach Burnout Inventory (MBI):** gold standard for depth; best used for program evaluation or major redesigns (Maslach et al., 2018).
- **Moral Injury Symptom Scale – Health Professionals (MISS-HP):** captures values-based injury not detected in standard burnout tools (Mantri et al., 2020).

HOW TO MEASURE ORGANIZATION

Units can burn out. Use four frames (Shanafelt & Noseworthy, 2017):

1. **Foundation: Are processes clear and consistent?**
2. **People: Are staff resourced, connected, and supported?**
3. **Environment: Is it psychologically safe to speak up?**
4. **Purpose: Does the work still feel like it matters?**

Trends matter more than points. Tie well-being data to operational metrics—turnover, time-to-fill, sick calls, and incident types.

LEADER MOVES THAT WILL CHANGE BEHAVIOR

Pick 2-3 instruments—then make them fit the work. One brief monthly pulse to flag risk and route help; one deeper instrument once or twice a year to track change. Time-box both. Two minutes for the pulse. Ten to twelve minutes for the deeper read. Offer paper for units without easy computer access and a hosted link for everyone else. Brief is not "lite." Brief is repeatable.

Write privacy rules a human can understand—then honor them in public. Specify who accesses raw data, how it is stored, and prohibited actions. Do not ask about diagnoses. Focus on current impairment. Host off the network if you can. Offer external counseling that never routes through a badge—present results in de-identified aggregates with safe group sizes. Use results for internal improvement only. Please put it in writing.

Close the loop in seven days. Data without action is worse than silence. After each pulse, managers share a one-page "we heard / we did" with dated line items. "East lot lights replaced." "Assignments flexed after violent incident." "Paused one low-value documentation task for two weeks while we evaluate." Keep it small and visible. A short loop builds more trust than a long speech. **Loop rule:** 7 days = slight change; 30 days = measured result + next step.

In serial crisis conditions, loops must be shorter, smaller, and more visible. You cannot wait a quarter for results when another hurricane or surge may arrive next month. That is why the 7-day micro loop and 30-day macro loop matter—they turn data into protection fast enough to matter.

Put well-being where decisions live. If burnout links to errors, LOS, and satisfaction, then it belongs on the same dashboard that runs the hospital. Pair a well-being trend with a quality metric and a people metric by unit. Show slopes, not just points. Set quarterly goals that a unit can feel (vacancy, time-to-fill, sick-call patterns), and tie dollars to levers that move those slopes.

Select some individuals to guide the discussion. Supervisors are not therapists and do not need to be. Please give them a two-question check-in script, a ten-minute grief-huddle format, and a clear handoff route. Teach them what to say when someone is not okay and how to protect a short decompression block without punishing the rest of the team. Psychological safety is not a poster. It is a hundred small conversations where people learn that telling the truth will not cost them.

PITFALLS AND TRADEOFFS TO BE AWARE OF

Survey theater. If people take time to answer and nothing happens, trust drops below zero. Keep your 7-day micro loop and 30-day macro loop and hit both every time.

Weaponized metrics. If a red score gets someone managed harder, your following dataset will be fiction. Put in writing that well-being data drives resources and design changes, not discipline. Address performance issues separately. Do not wave a well-being chart while you do it.

One-size-fits-all instruments. Burnout and moral injury overlap, but they are not the same. Use burnout tools for exhaustion and disconnection; use MISS-HP when the harm is values-based and words like betrayal, shame, and blocked ethics are in the air.

Privacy theater. Posters about confidentiality do not matter if IT can see raw strings or managers can back-solve identities from free text. Aggregate to safe group sizes. Strip identifiers. Host outside the hospital network if possible. Publish a one-page data governance policy and keep it current.

Survey fatigue. If every quarter feels like another box to check, participation will crash. Keep pulses brief. Retire questions that are not changing decisions. Show how last month's answer changed next month's work.

Ignoring nights, rural sites, and per diem staff. If you collect answers only on the day shift or only at the flagship, your read is partial, and your solutions will miss the people who carry the heaviest load. Put a paper option by the time clock, a QR in the break room, and give people time on the clock to answer.

Pretty dashboards that do not run decisions. The right audience for well-being trends is the same audience that reviews safety, quality, and cost. If your well-being lines are not in the C-suite weekly readout, you are still doing side work.

CHANGES TO EXPECT ONCE YOU START MEASURING

People stop speaking in general. "Morale is low" becomes "fatigue and numbness climb after pediatric codes, and schedule flexibility within fourteen days lowers both." "The lab is drowning" becomes "courier timing is breaking night shift; one re-sequenced run cut rejects by a third."

The C-Suite gets a line of sight into how well-being connects to safety and cost without compromising staff well-being. Managers get a permission structure to make humane decisions. New graduates learn early that help is part of the job. Veterans see policy, not cupcakes.

Your language shifts, too. You stop asking, "Who is burned out?" and start asking, "Where is the work injuring people, and which part of the system can we change next?" That question pulls you out of blame and into design.

A NOTE ON HOMEMADE SCALES AND SHARING DATA

You do not need to build your survey from scratch. The time you spend arguing over wording is time you could spend fixing conditions. Use validated tools built for healthcare (WBI, PFI, MBI, MISS-HP). Spend your energy on closing loops.

You are not publishing dirty laundry. You are doing internal quality improvement as a leading indicator of safety and cost. The ACGME expects attention to well-being. The National Plan urges de-identification and internal use of data to drive system-level change. Clinicians will back you if you protect them and then act.

WHAT SUCCESS LOOKS LIKE

You will not get a standing ovation. You will get fewer sick calls on Mondays after hard weekends. A lift in "I feel safe speaking up" on units where managers run the grief-huddle script.

Fewer short-notice resignations. Safety events that shift from injury to learning. Jokes again: the kind that mean people still like each other. Moreover, a chief financial officer stops seeing well-being as a soft cost and starts seeing it as a lever that moves turnover, travel staff spending, and errors. The literature backs that link. Your numbers will, too.

Sometimes the numbers do not lead to exhaustion. This reflects betrayal: recognizing the right action but being obstructed by the system. In the chapters ahead, we will thread moral distress through the culture and leadership moves, so you can act on it without launching a separate program.

9

WHAT WOULD IT TAKE
To Build Something Better – After Everything

One of my favorite definitions of culture is "the way we do things around here." If that is true, then every healthcare system has a culture, whether we intentionally shape it or not. If we want a different outcome, we need a different culture. However, culture change is not magic. It is not a branding strategy or a reorganization. It is not an app or an after-hours yoga class. It takes time, trust, and actual power-sharing.

When I speak to organizations about building sustainable cultures, I tell them to start by identifying their pain points and pressure valves. Where do people feel unseen, unheard, or unsafe? Where are people checking out, emotionally or physically? That is where you focus. That is where change starts.

If you do not create new systems, people will return to old ones, even if they are harmful. Humans will default to the familiar norms, especially in high-pressure environments. That means leaders must design for vulnerability. You must create space for honest conversations, and back them up with actions and resources.

SERIAL DISASTERS CHANGE THE STARTING POINT

If Chapter 8 showed how to read the harm, this chapter turns the wrench — but the wrench here is for a workforce already running on depleted reserves. In regular times, change management assumes the baseline of moderate stress. Serial disasters result in compounded depletion, moral injury, and disaster fatigue.

This is not a "wellness initiative." It is a **stabilization and rebuilding plan** that must:

- Make honesty safe in a climate of distrust.
- Put structured recovery time into operations, not afterthoughts.
- Protect moral agency in moments when the system pulls the wrong way.

The difference is urgency: every day you delay relief, you accelerate exits — and in a disaster-compounded workforce, those exits are permanent.

LESSONS IN MISGUIDED LEADERSHIP

Despite years of clinical training and experience working through major disasters, I have made mistakes as a leader. One moment I will never forget came after the 2016 floods in Baton Rouge. Two of my staff members lost their homes. Our Academic Affairs team, always a group that rises, jumped into action. We helped remove water-logged belongings, raised money through a raffle, and scheduled volunteers to assist with cleanup and recovery. It felt like we were doing everything right.

However, within weeks, I started noticing signs of fatigue across the team. Deadlines were slipping. People were quieter. The same staff who had stepped up were now shutting down.

Moreover, I did what too many leaders do: I ordered pizza. Once a week. I thought it was a nice gesture. It was not enough.

I returned to a leadership strategy that has always grounded me: one-on-one conversations. However, this time, I did not want to talk about productivity. I sat with every team member and asked a simple question: "How are you really doing?"

That decision changed everything.

What I learned was sobering. The team members who had flooded felt overwhelmed, torn between gratitude for the support of their peers and the endless paperwork of FEMA forms and insurance claims. They were grateful for the response of their peers, but things were moving so fast, and they did not have time to grieve. Others were physically depleted after working full-time and spending weekends gutting their homes or the homes of colleagues. What was meant to be helpful had become one more thing to manage.

I heard the most consistent theme. People needed *time*—not platitudes or pizza. Just time to rest, to rebuild, to be with their families. So, we tried something different: we moved to a four ten-hour day workweek. It gave everyone an extra day each week to recover. We did it for four months.

Years later, that one shift still comes up in conversations. It did not cost the organization a dime. Productivity improved. Morale stabilized. However, most importantly, people felt seen. Leadership is about listening, adjusting, and creating space for people to heal.

This experience taught me something I carry forward to this day: Intentional recovery takes more than intention—it takes adaptation. Moreover, it starts when we stop assuming we know what people need and start asking them instead.

CULTURE REQUIRES INVESTMENT

Cultural change requires staffing. It requires a budget. It requires leadership. It requires the humility to ask people, "What do you need to be well?" and believe their answers.

You cannot demand "resilience" from people while denying them basic workplace dignity. You cannot talk about equity without examining who gets protected, promoted, and paid. You cannot expect clinicians to feel safe in a system that punishes vulnerability and rewards overwork.

Details define culture. In whom gets time off and who does not. Whether new parents feel supported. Whether team members get feedback or just evaluations. An error can be considered either a constructive opportunity for learning or a possible liability. In whom gets to ask questions without retaliation.

Implementing change often means analyzing patterns related to race, class, gender, and generational experiences. That is challenging work. However, it is also the real work of culture change. If your wellness program is not wrestling with structural inequality, it is just another way to make people feel broken.

WHAT IT TAKES

- **Leadership that listens** — and acts.
- **Ongoing funding,** not a single allocation.
- **Data that is transparent** — and tied to decisions.
- **Programs that speak to real pain**, not just performance.

The future of healthcare depends on how we care for the people who deliver it. We cannot wait for the crisis to force our hands. We must lead now, with clarity, compassion, and the courage to build something better.

The gap between knowing and doing is where cultural change so often stalls. We cannot afford that pause. Real progress is emerging in the field where leaders are stepping into the hard work of transformation — and showing us the path forward.

LESSONS FROM THE FIELD

Healing a healthcare system is not a theory. It is practice, evaluated in the field where lives are on the line and margins are thin. Across the country, hospitals and health systems have begun to confront the hidden costs of burnout, depletion, and fragmentation by experimenting with bold changes. Their stories carry lessons worth holding onto because they remind us that transformation is possible.

ERLANGER HEALTH SYSTEM: REDUCING BURDEN, EMPOWERING TEAMS

At Erlanger Health System in Tennessee, the challenge was not a lack of dedication, but rather a mountain of administrative work. Physicians and nurses were suffocating under fifteen different medical record systems. The move to consolidate into one system could have broken morale—but instead, Erlanger turned the transition into a moment of culture change.

They focused on three key goals: reducing the documentation burden, automating repetitive tasks, and enhancing **usability.** Electronic medical record templates and voice recognition reduced typing. Protocols empowered respiratory therapists to deliver inhaler therapy without waiting for physician orders. Discharge summaries began flowing automatically to outpatient providers.

The results were striking: 83% of encounters closed within

a day, refill authorizations dropped to just over one day, and providers reported spending more time with patients than with screens. This aligns with research showing that interventions reducing electronic health record (EHR) use can directly decrease stress and improve physician satisfaction (Shanafelt et al., 2016; Downing et al., 2018).

Erlanger redesigned its electronic health record processes to address physician burnout. By engaging frontline clinicians in workflow redesign, they reduced documentation burden and improved usability. This work was highlighted by the American Hospital Association's Physician Alliance as a best practice in reducing burnout through structural changes (AHA Physician Alliance, 2018; Becker's Hospital Review, 2019).

The lesson? Technology boosts efficiency when it is designed with human needs in mind, rather than forcing people to adapt.

MINNESOTA HOSPITAL ASSOCIATION: DATA AS A SURVIVAL TOOL

Minnesota took a different approach. With 142 hospitals across a vast and varied state, no single intervention could reach everyone. Instead, the Minnesota Hospital Association (MHA) asked a simple question: *Can we measure burnout at scale and act on what we learn?*

In 2016, the Minnesota Hospital Association launched a statewide survey of 13,000 clinicians, repeated annually, which revealed burnout levels of 34% compared to nearly 50% nationally. The survey reframed well-being as a measurable quality metric, spurring three-quarters of health systems to create action plans within six months. The AHA and Becker's have cited Minnesota's approach as a model of system-level accountability for clinician well-being (Minnesota Hospital Association, 2017; Becker's Hospital Review, 2018).

The lesson? Measured metrics usually receive more

attention. By treating burnout like a quality metric—not a private shame—Minnesota reframed well-being as part of the Quadruple Aim (Bodenheimer & Sinsky, 2014). Their work shows us that when leaders take measurement seriously, change becomes a collective project, not a personal burden.

TRINITY HEALTH: REDESIGNING ROLES WITH TRUST

Sometimes healing begins with a single line of policy. At Trinity Health, one of the nation's largest Catholic hospital systems, a policy on documentation had quietly stolen hours of physician time. By restricting Registered Nurses and Medical Assistants from contributing to patient histories, the burden fell entirely on physicians.

At Trinity Health, leaders revised documentation policies to enable Registered Nurses and Medical Assistants to contribute to patient histories, thereby reducing after-hours charting for physicians. Encounter closures improved, patient satisfaction rose, and burnout declined. This change, cited in both AHA Physician Alliance case studies and Becker's reporting, illustrates how policy-level redesign can directly ease clinician burden (AHA Physician Alliance, 2019; Becker's Hospital Review, 2019).

However, the most important lesson came from a physician leader who said, *"We must build trust among providers to let go of some control and allow others to be part of the care team."* Trust was not just a cultural virtue; it became a strategic operational approach for sustainability. This reflects evidence that team-based care models both improve outcomes and reduce physician stress (Willard-Grace et al., 2014; Sinsky et al., 2017).

The lesson? Sustainable redesign requires trust – sharing work, sharing responsibility, and sharing credit.

FRANCISCAN MISSIONARIES OF OUR LADY HEALTH SYSTEM

When E.J. Kuiper became CEO of this Baton Rouge–based system in 2024, he directly acknowledged the depleted workforce. His central leadership principle was simple—**take care of the people who care for patients, and performance will follow**.

Within a single year, FMOLHS achieved an extraordinary turnaround. The health system expanded benefits, launched leadership development initiatives, and prioritized visible recognition of its staff. Kuiper modeled presence, walking the halls of hospitals and clinics, creating a culture of listening and responsiveness. The results were profound: turnover dropped below 12%, engagement scores climbed, and patient experience improved. Several FMOLHS hospitals also earned **"A" Safety Grades from the Leapfrog Group**, demonstrating that investments in people translated directly into safer, higher-quality care.

This cultural shift coincided with a dramatic financial recovery. FMOLHS reported a net income in FY 2024 that represented a gain of more than 150% over the previous year, reflecting one of the most dramatic financial turnarounds in the system's history. Growth in operating revenue and disciplined cost management reflected how workforce investment fueled stability and performance. The American Hospital Association (AHA) and Becker's both featured FMOLHS's turnaround as evidence that workforce investment fuels safety, quality, and financial strength (AHA, 2024; Becker's Hospital Review, 2024).

As Kuiper explained, "You can have beautiful buildings and technology, but it is the people who create the healing environment." FMOLHS serves as a potent reminder that when leaders prioritize employees, organizations not only restore morale but also achieve measurable improvements in quality, safety, and financial strength.

The lesson? When leaders prioritize people, financial strength and high-quality outcomes follow.

WELLSPAN YORK HOSPITAL
LISTENING FIRST

In Pennsylvania, WellSpan York Hospital started its journey by asking physicians two simple questions: *How can we improve your life? What can we do to change?* Within 36 hours, 40% of respondents had responded. Leaders implemented tangible changes: a redesigned physician lounge, buddy systems, and a leadership academy. This approach, as described in both Becker's Hospital Review and AHA Physician Alliance reports, demonstrates how listening to and acting on clinician feedback is a direct intervention that fosters engagement and trust (AHA Physician Alliance, 2018; Becker's Hospital Review, 2019).

From those comments came rapid interventions: a valet service for doctors rushing in for emergencies, a redesigned lounge with healthy food and fitness space, a buddy system for new physicians, and a Physician Leadership Academy to prepare the next generation.

The lesson? Sometimes the act of listening itself is an intervention. When physicians saw their feedback turned into action, engagement grew, retention improved, and leadership pipelines expanded. Well-being stopped being an afterthought and became part of the hospital's identity. These findings echo research demonstrating that organizational responsiveness to clinician feedback is strongly associated with reduced burnout and higher engagement (Shanafelt & Noseworthy, 2017).

The lesson? Listening is not passive; it is an intervention that builds trust, drives engagement, and seeds sustainable cultural change.

NOVANT HEALTH
COURAGE TO REFRAME

I remember speaking with a colleague from North Carolina who told me about a decisive shift in her health system, Novant Health. Despite being a leading healthcare employer, disengagement among physicians and nurses was increasing.

That was when their Chief Human Experience Officer, a practicing physician, made a bold move. He had personally walked through the fire of burnout, uncovering in coaching the patterns that had been undoing him: perfectionism, people-pleasing, and overcommitment. He refused to stop at personal healing. Instead, he chose to scale that clarity to others.

His pitch was radical in its simplicity: a leadership development program that looked nothing like traditional wellness offerings. It was immersive, personal, and emotionally honest. The goal was not to fix anyone—it was to reconnect clinicians with why they had entered medicine in the first place.

The result? A three-day coaching-based program that now has more than 2,000 graduates. Participants describe it as life-changing. Both AHA and Becker's highlight Novant's work as an example of courageous reframing that reconnects clinicians with their purpose (AHA Physician Alliance, 2020; Becker's Hospital Review, 2021). Moreover, the system changed as well.

Engagement scores skyrocketed. Teams redesigned care around shared purpose. Scribes were engaged to alleviate the demands of documentation. Primary care clinics added behavioral health services. New employees were paired with program graduates as mentors. Wellness was no longer optional; it was operational.

Most striking of all, they did not call it "burnout recovery." They called it **leadership development.** That was clever branding *and* a cultural reframe. It said: *"This is not about weakness. This is about taking ownership of your life."*

That story stuck with me because it proved what I have long believed: we do not lack the ideas to fix healthcare—we lack the courage to implement them. Research confirms that leadership behaviors have a measurable impact on clinician well-being; a Mayo Clinic study found that every one-point increase in a supervisor's leadership score correlated with a 3% decrease in burnout and a 9% increase in satisfaction (Shanafelt et al., 2015). Novant's work is a living example of those findings.

The lesson? Courageous leadership reframes well-being from a deficit model into a source of strength and purpose.

THE RENEWAL LAB
BUILT FOR DISASTER-COMPOUNDED RECOVERY

Call the system Riverbend Health. Mid-sized, multi-hospital, urban and rural. The last five years have been a rolling disaster film: hurricanes, wildfires, a mass shooting, cyber downtime, and three significant surges. Traveler nurse spending ballooned, huddles got snappish, and people said the quiet part aloud: *"I do not think I can do this again."*

Instead of another morale campaign, they built the **Renewal Lab**, designed for serial disaster recovery:

Part One: Lead humans through the aftermath. Modeled partly on Novant's program, leaders spent three days in coaching-heavy immersion — practicing grief huddles, power-sharing boundaries, and how to communicate "what is changing and here is the budget line that moved." In disaster recovery, trust comes from showing receipts.

Part Two: Move money toward relief. A work redesign fund for units to buy back time or safety — like Erlanger's scribes, HCA's automation, or Trinity's MA role expansion. Rules: every dollar must reduce workload or increase safety, and units must post the "time we got back" like a safety win.

Part Three: Wrap policy around truth and privacy. Borrowing from MHA's transparency model, they committed to "we heard/ we did" updates within seven days of each monthly pulse check. Counseling access moved off-network with anonymous booking codes because post-disaster trust is brittle.

THREADS THAT BIND

What unites Erlanger, the Minnesota Hospital Association, Trinity Health, Novant Health, and Franciscan Missionaries of Our Lady Health System is not geography, size, or governance. The thread that binds them is a recognition that **healing systems begin by healing their people**.

Each story shows that recovery is possible when leaders resist the urge to fix symptoms and instead invest in the workforce itself. Using coaching leadership, strengths-based programs, or holistic benefits, these organizations recognized that excellence is only possible with a restored workforce.

The outcomes were strikingly consistent: improved retention, stronger engagement, safer care, higher patient satisfaction, and even financial turnarounds. In each case, what appeared at first to be a workforce challenge was, in fact, an opportunity. Leaders who listened deeply, invested boldly, and acted with humility unlocked the most resilient force in healthcare—the dedication of the people who choose to keep showing up.

This is the lesson for all of us: culture is not abstract. Leadership decisions shape or diminish it each day. When leaders choose to put the well-being of their people at the center, they not only rebuild morale but also create systems where patients, families, and communities thrive.

WHAT THE STRONGEST EVIDENCE – AND HARD EXPERIENCE – SAY WORKS

The environment changes outcomes. Healthy professional practice environments, adequate staffing, and strong local leadership correlate with lower mortality and better retention. Post-disaster, minor friction points want to become break points, making environmental fixes even more urgent.

Voice is a survival tool. The Minnesota Hospital Association's statewide burnout survey made it safe for leaders to name and address drivers of distress and required action plans within six months. That is the cadence you need when disaster cycles keep repeating.

Workflow relief beats slogans. Erlanger Health reduced EHR clicks, delegated routine care tasks to trained staff, and used scribes strategically. In a disaster-recovery context, those freed minutes are the difference between a clinician staying for the next shift or calling a recruiter.

Cut the waste before retraining. HCA Healthcare's documentation redesign eliminated low-value fields and automated vital signs capture, saving nurses an hour per shift. Following a surge or crisis, that hour may be explicitly allocated for decompression or skill restoration.

Team-based care is a disaster recovery multiplier. Trinity Health expanded the RN and MA scope to include initiating HPI documentation. That shift, paired with clear physician validation, prevents bottlenecks and keeps patients moving through strained systems.

Leadership capacity matters most when leaders are as tired as their teams. Novant Health built a leadership development program with executive coaching at its core. In serial disaster recovery, this kind of leader capacity-building is non-negotiable.

Taken together, these lessons point to a simple truth: recovery is not about inspiration; it is about infrastructure. If you cannot see it, track it, and respond in real time, the most substantial evidence will never translate into daily practice. That is why we built the Tuesday Scoreboard — a recovery-focused dashboard that makes well-being, safety, and workload visible to staff and leaders alike.

THE TUESDAY SCOREBOARD (BUILT FOR RECOVERY)

- **People:** vacancy; time-to-fill; sick-call patterns post-disaster; overtime/traveler hours.
- **Safety & Quality:** incident types, violence reports, near-misses.
- **Experience:** one patient-comment signal (*"care felt rushed?"*), one staff-voice signal (*"I feel safe speaking up"*).
- **Burden:** after-hours EHR time; disaster-response debrief completions; supply-hunt minutes.
- **Cadence:** monthly; staff see it before executives; every posting includes "we heard → we did" with dates.

Tracking the right signals is only half the work. A scoreboard tells you where the strain is showing up, but it does not tell you what to do next. That is where the Disaster Recovery Intervention Map comes in — a practical guide that links core moves to real-world case studies, post-disaster adaptations, and the evidence base behind them.

DISASTER RECOVERY INTERVENTION MAP

Core Move	Case Study Example	Post-Disaster Adaptation	Evidence Base
Name Reality & Shared Power in Public	**Minnesota Hospital Association – Burnout survey + required action plans**	High-risk units hold monthly "disaster debrief" town halls. Post results and fixes before C-Suite review	Edmondson AC. *Adm Sci Q.* 1999;44(2):350-383. West MA et al. *BMJ Qual Saf.* 2014;23:153–161.
Hard-wire Decompression into Operations	**Novant Health – Leadership development & resilience coaching**	Paid decompression blocks tied to defined disaster exposures; cross-trained staff cover relief.	Shanafelt TD et al. *Ann Surg.* 2010;251(6):995–1000. National Academies. *Taking Action Against Clinician Burnout.* 2019.
Redesign Work Before You Retrain People	**Erlanger – EHR streamlining, task delegation HCA – Documentation redesign & automation**	Post-disaster: eliminate non-essential documentation, automate vitals, delegate stable follow-ups.	Sinsky CA et al. *Ann Intern Med.* 2016;165(11):753-760. Adler-Milstein J, Huckman RS. *Health Aff.* 2013;32(11):1960-1967.
Make Psychological Safety a Managerial Skill	**Novant Health – Coaching immersion communication & presence**	Leaders trained for grief huddles, disaster debriefs, and moral distress conversations.	O'Donovan R, McAuliffe E. BMC Health Serv Res. 2020;20:810. Dekker S. Just Culture. 3rd ed. 2017.
Invest in the Messy Middle	**Trinity – Expanded MA & RN scope to free physician time**	After disasters: mid-level leaders get micro-budgets + coverage authority to pilot relief projects.	West CP et al. *Implement Sci.* 2014;9:98. Shanafelt TD, Noseworthy JH. *Mayo Clin Proc.* 2017;92(1):129-146.

However, maps and metrics can only take us so far. In the thick of serial disasters, the breaking point is not just exhaustion; it is moral distress. When clinicians are forced, again, to choose between two bad options or to watch patients suffer from a lack of resources, the wound goes deeper than fatigue. It cuts at purpose, identity, and the very reason people entered medicine. That is why confronting moral distress head-on is not optional; it is survival.

MORAL DISTRESS IN SERIAL DISASTERS

In disaster recovery, moral distress increases when repeated obstacles prevent doing what is right, such as unavailable ventilators, disrupted evacuations, or difficult resource allocation. The playbook: "Where did we have to choose the least-harm option this week?"

- **Name the event:** 10-minute huddles separate from grief debriefs.
- **Escalate fast:** Unit → dyad→ ethics on-call (24–48h)→ exec sponsor.
- **Temporary relief:** Assignments flexed, alternative pathways allowed.
- **Close the loop:** Provide either the solution or an explanation for why it remains unresolved.

THE TRADEOFFS YOU MUST NAME

Real recovery costs: coverage for decompression, IT investment for automation, letting go of sacred-cow processes. The traps are predictable: wellness theater, leadership whiplash, equity theater, metric gaming, privacy theater. In a serial disaster context, the fallout is faster — because credibility is already thin.

Name the tradeoffs. Publish the rationale. People do not need perfection. They need proof that this time, Tuesday will be different.

10

LEADING THE REBUILD:

Tools to Restore Trust, Energy, and Well-Being

The after-action meeting started late because the ED was short of two techs and a registrar. Someone wheeled in a cart of muffins. The COO thanked "our heroes," read the incident report, and asked for lessons learned. A nurse said nights still did not have a way to call security without leaving the pod. A respiratory therapist said, "We ran out of SpO_2 probes at 3 a.m., again." A resident said he had not slept. The room nodded.

The COO promised, "We will look into it." By Tuesday, the muffins were stale, and the probes came in without labels. People stopped talking—not because they did not care, but because nothing moved. In a crisis-tested system, which is what a dying trust looks like.

After **serial disasters,** hurricanes, floods, ransomware downtime, mass casualty events, and COVID surges, the cumulative impact is significant. The literature on disaster psychology, occupational trauma, and health system resilience makes it clear: the half-life of trust shortens with each hit, recovery windows shrink, and conventional "change management" playbooks do not fit (NASEM, 2019; Brooks et al., 2020). To rebuild, leadership must get **trauma-informed and operational**: make honesty safe, move money and rules where the harm lives, and hard-wire recovery the way you hard-wire infection control.

That means:

- **Clear safety signals** (physical and psychological) every shift.
- **Radical transparency** when news is bad.
- **Peer support embedded in workflow**, not bolted on.
- **Supervisors trained to read trauma responses** without punishment.
- **Real agency at the department/unit level** to act on hazards and moral concerns.

This is not about pep talks or apps. It is about redesigning how **power, time, and attention** move through the building so trust, energy, and care can return.

This is how trust erodes — not in one dramatic collapse, but in small unmet promises that pile up until silence feels safer than speaking. The question is what breaks that cycle. The answer is not muffins or slogans, but evidence. Both literature and real-world field experience show us where recovery gains traction and what truly keeps clinicians, patients, and systems alive overall.

WHAT THE LITERATURE AND FIELD EVIDENCE SAY

- **Better nurse work environments save lives.** Adequate RN staffing, strong unit-level leadership, and collaborative team climate correlate with lower mortality and failure-to-rescue rates—across normal and post-disaster conditions (Aiken et al., 2014; Daugherty Biddison et al., 2019).
- **Voice is a survival tool.** Teams with psychological safety report hazards earlier, adapt faster, and sustain performance under pressure (Edmondson, 1999). Silence after disasters delays correction until the subsequent failure.

- **Burnout is a safety issue.** Extensive national studies show clinician burnout and fatigue independently predict self-reported medical errors—even after adjusting for safety grades (Shanafelt et al., 2010; Tawfik et al., 2018).
- **Embedded support works.** Structured reflective forums—such as Schwartz Rounds or in-shift grief huddles—improve well-being and empathy when built into the work week. Post-disaster recovery research shows that accessible, in-place support reduces PTSD symptoms and speeds functional recovery (Watson et al., 2011).

AFTER THE STORM: A DIFFERENT PLAYBOOK

Call the system **Cypress Health**. Mid-sized, hurricane belt, two hospitals, a sprawl of clinics. In three years: two floods, a ransomware shutdown, and two COVID surges that pulled senior nurses off the schedule for good. Turnover up. Traveling nurses are crushing the budget. People were not angry; they were empty.

Amid the exhaustion, a new chief of staff stepped in with a different lens. An ICU physician who had personally walked through burnout and found his way back, he offered a blunt prescription: "Treat trust like a clinical pathway." The plan was simple and disciplined- four priorities, ninety days, each with an accountable owner.

What followed were four priorities, each backed by specific action items, designed to rebuild trust in the everyday mechanics of care.

1. **Safety as a signal, not a poster.**

- Security rounds shifted to cover high-risk times and locations (shift change, night lots).
- Facilities fixed a long-broken night-shift badge reader.

- ED added a two-minute "red flags" pass at huddle: safety concerns, supply gaps, or violent-patient alerts named aloud with an owner attached.

2. Truth on a cadence.

- COO livestream every Wednesday, same script: what is known, unknown, changing this week, on deck next week, and what slipped—with reasons.
- When rumors about service cuts started, leadership showed the actual decision tree and timeline.

3. Help where the work is.

- Peer responders trained in Psychological First Aid (per WHO guidelines) assigned to high-exposure units.
- Pager number posted next to code cart.
- Ten-minute grief-huddle script on every unit clipboard.
- Managers ask in 1:1s: "What hit you last week? What would help this week?"
- Confidential counseling booked via off-network link.

4. Power and time.

- Unit-level redesigned budgets, restricted to buying back minutes or adding safety.
- Examples: ED killed a legacy triage rule wasting clinical judgment; med-surg hired evening supply runners; busiest clinic piloted scribes; nights evaluated four-tens plus recovery day after "heavy exposure" weeks.

WHAT CHANGED IN 90 DAYS AT CYPRESS HEALTH

The impact showed up quickly. Night-shift assault reports went down, not because people stopped filing them, but because security started showing up where the risk lived. The scribe pilot proved itself almost overnight, cutting after-hours charting by forty minutes a day. Expansion was approved on the spot. Resignations slowed. Staff surveys on stagnant units showed a slight increase in "I feel safe speaking up."

Moreover, it was not just the metric. A charge nurse said out loud, "I feel less alone." That mattered. The CFO still grumbled about the peer-responder budget line, but even he could see the connection: less turnover, fewer traveling nurses. The plan did not stick because it was inspiring. It stuck because it was mechanical—fixes people could see and feel.

WHAT MOVES THE NEEDLE IN SERIAL DISASTER RECOVERY

Across disasters, the patterns became clear. Safety must be treated like a design problem, not a poster on the wall. Fix one tangible hazard every week and publish it like an infection-control win.

Truth works best when it is on a schedule. A predictable cadence of updates, even when the news is bad, steadies people more than sporadic briefings ever will.

Support must be embedded where the work is happening. A peer responder trained in Psychological First Aid is only effective if they are visible in the shift, not bolted on from the outside.

Redesign the work before you retrain people. Strip out the low-value tasks, unblock the bottlenecks, then celebrate the win. Furthermore, train supervisors for trauma literacy and just culture, because recovery demands leaders who can recognize hypervigilance, numbing, and collapse—and respond without causing more harm.

THE MORAL AGENCY PATHWAY (90-DAY BUILD)

Restoring moral agency required more than encouragement; it needed a pathway people could trust. First came clarity in policy: impairment would be defined by current function, not a lifetime diagnosis, explained on a single page so staff understood their rights. A short, off-network reporting route was created for blocked-care events, bypassing the usual bureaucracy.

Ethics support was made real, with an on-call ethicist available around the clock and empowered to act within 48 hours. Micro-budgets and schedule flexibility gave units the tools to address moral injuries in real time, whether that meant reassigning a nurse after a traumatic event or funding a quick fix to relieve a recurring pain point.

Every week, leaders published updates that included numbers, response times, and a visible thread of *"we heard/we did."* Guardrails of just culture were posted openly, along with a clear escalation ladder and a promise of zero retaliation. It was not a theory; it was a structure, designed to restore dignity where it had been lost.

WHERE THIS CAN GO SIDEWAYS

However, even firm plans can fail if leaders miss the point. Performative gestures—like rolling out wellness apps or bringing muffins without addressing workload—only deepen cynicism. Leadership whiplash, with big speeches followed by no funding, erodes credibility faster than silence.

Privacy "theater" is another trap: if counseling sessions or micro-report data can be traced back to individuals, trust collapses instantly. Moreover, metrics can be played; boosting engagement scores while ignoring unresolved hazards is not a recovery of its spin. Each misstep reminds people why they stopped speaking up in the first place.

EQUITY IN RECOVERY

One more reality: serial disasters never land evenly. Nights, rural hospitals, new parents, and dispersed teams often feel the strain the most and benefit the least from "big wins." Recovery must be designed for those edges.

That meant childcare stipends or swaps for staff with young families, and tele-debriefs for remote or rural teams who otherwise missed the chance to process. It meant parking and security at times and places where people felt vulnerable. Moreover, it meant intentional mentorship—matching people deliberately rather than leaving it to chance.

Building for the margins made the system stronger for everyone.

PATTERN IS THE PLAN

Culture does not shift because of a retreat. It shifts when the organization sees patterns it can trust—steady, visible rhythms that prove change is real. One hazard is eliminated every week. Protect recovery time after the hits. Shared authority where decisions happen. That cadence becomes the new culture.

Sometimes the deepest wound is not operational at all; it is a fracture of values. That is moral distress, and no amount of pizza parties or extra PTO will mend it. The only way forward is to restore moral agency. Think of it as the cast and the rehab plan: the structure and the work that allow healing to take hold.

11

WE DO NOT JUST REBUILD SYSTEMS.
We Restore People

I have worked in healthcare long enough to know we rarely get pauses. The next patient, the next call, the next crisis is always waiting. However, before you turn the page or sprint into the next initiative, sit with this: healthcare is not what it was twenty years ago. Not before Katrina. Not before COVID. Not after the last flood, fire, hack, or surge.

The differences are not only new policies or reconfigured organizational charts. The people are different. Some are stronger. Some are hurting. Many are both. No one stayed untouched.

We know how to rebuild buildings. We have ripped out drywall, sanitized rooms, patched roofs, reopened clinics, and ordered ribbon cuttings with a deadline. We have stood in parking lots handing out scrubs from cardboard boxes and running EDs off generator power. We know organization; we can make a floor hum again.

What we skip, because it is harder to see on a dashboard, is the emotional infrastructure. The human core. The part of the workforce that holds everything else together. If that fractures, everything else follows.

This book is not a checklist or a pep talk. It is an invitation to lead differently and to rebuild from the inside out. Burnout is not a character flaw. Trauma is not a private problem. They are warning lights in the system. Ignore them and you lose staff, safety, and the mission that brought you here.

The national momentum is real. The National Plan for Health Workforce Well-Being includes recommendations to reduce administrative burden, promote a just culture, and establish well-being as a core metric rather than an ancillary program. The field is finally saying aloud that well-being is a core condition of safe care. Plans exist. Toolkits exist. Some have already appeared here. However, plans do not restore people. People restore people when leaders give them time, cover, and permission to heal.

Here is the part I want to land with weight: healing is possible.

I have seen it. In post-Katrina emergency rooms, nurses laughed again after months of tight jaws. In ICUs, where the jokes came back without being cruel. In clinics where a manager finally said, "Go home at four. I have the phones," and meant it. In boardrooms where a CFO learned to ask, "What did the night shift say?" before approving a spend. Wellness stops being a slogan when the room can point to something that moved.

WHAT YOU HAVE JUST WALKED THROUGH

If you have read this far, you have tolerated blunt truths. Silence is often seen as "professional" until it leads to someone vanishing. **Resilience without recovery is not strength at all; it is denial disguised in a scrub top.** You have met Dana and the "we heard / we did" loop. You have watched a composite system run grief huddles, fix parking lights, move courier times, and keep two nurses who were on the brink of leaving. You have measured the harm, not to punish, but to route care. You have named moral distress for what it is: a fracture of values that does not respond to pizza or PTO.

None of this was about perfection. It was about telling the truth and then changing the room to match.

WHAT WE MUST REMEMBER

Change is not tidy. You will meet resistance from structures that profit from sameness and from colleagues who wear exhaustion like a badge. You will hear the old refrains: "We tried that." "Not in my budget." "What if everyone asks for time?" You will feel your doubt.

Make the move anyway. Culture shifts when one leader chooses to act like a human in public and continues to do so long enough for others to copy. It sustains when that choice becomes contagious.

A GLIMPSE OF WHAT IS POSSIBLE

Imagine a department where morning huddles include a check for anything heavy on the floor, and when something is heavy, the next step is cover, not platitudes. Imagine a hospital that celebrates mental health days with the same seriousness it uses to honor perfect attendance. Imagine a CEO who opens staff meetings with, "What do you need from me this week to make the work safer?" Imagine a medical school where emotional regulation and just culture sit next to clinical reasoning on the syllabus.

These are not fantasies. They are happening in pockets, then in programs, then in policy.

Where do they start? Small.

One honest conversation that does not end with "I am fine." One leader refuses to answer emails after 7 p.m. and tells the room why. One organization that budgets for mental health access the way it does for MRI magnets, with a line item and a maintenance plan. One system that stops calling a crisis "unprecedented" and starts building capacity for the next one on purpose.

FIVE COMMITMENTS TO CARRY FORWARD

From these lessons came a simple pledge—five commitments that leaders can carry forward, no matter the setting. They are not slogans or wellness posters; they are behaviors to practice, shift after shift, if trust and resilience are going to hold.

1. I will ask, "How are you doing?" and wait for the answer. That means silence that is not weaponized and a follow-up that is not performative. If the answer is "not okay," your next move is to route support, not advice.

2. I will treat rest and recovery as a responsibility, not a reward. If a team carried three pediatric codes in a week, the question is when their decompression block lands, not whether they "earned it."

3. I will acknowledge moral distress and seek solutions, not silence. When policy forces people to choose between what they know is right and what the system permits, leaders change the policy or escalate with receipts. You do not gaslight the floor.

4. I will advocate for well-being like any critical clinical tool. You would not expect a catheter without sterile gloves. Do not expect safe care without time to recover and a way to speak up.

5. I will not confuse professionalism with emotional suppression. A steady tone is helpful in a crisis, but a flat culture is a brittle one. Let people be people, and the system will last longer.

HONORING QUIET WORK

You have already been doing this, quietly, with zero fanfare. The hallway debriefs after the impossible case. The text that says, "I picked up your notes. Go home." The nurse who carries extra pens because she remembers what it is like to ask for one and feels small. The registrar who learns the names of the security guards and tells them when the lot feels off. The resident who sits with a family five minutes longer than the schedule allows.

That is leadership. That is restoration. That is how the rebuild begins.

WHAT RESTORATION LOOKS LIKE IN PRACTICE

Restoration is concrete. It lives in calendars, budgets, ratios, and scripts.

It looks like a ten-minute grief huddle after loss, held on every shift for three days, led by someone trained to hold space without turning the room into therapy. It looks like a red flag pass at the start of the huddle, where people can name a safety issue and see an owner write it down with a date. It looks like a small redesign fund in the hands of the unit, with one rule: spend it on buying back minutes or safety. It looks like schedule autonomy that is not cosmetic: four 10-hour shifts where the fourth is genuinely lighter after a "heavy exposure" week, not a 12-hour shift in disguise.

The restoration question is designed similarly to a credentialing inquiry, focusing on present impairment rather than a lifetime diagnosis. This is an external portal for booking counseling, and no badge ping is needed. It looks like a seven-day loop: data on Monday, slight change by Friday, public readout the following week.

Restoration looks like a manager who knows how to read a nervous system under strain and who can say, "You are not failing. Your brain is telling you, you have been under threat too long. Let us repair conditions, not your character." It looks like a director who takes heat from finance and still backs a team's decision to slow down after a violent incident. It looks like an executive who says "I do not know" in public and returns at the time promised with what has changed.

WHAT GETS IN THE WAY AND HOW YOU WALK THROUGH IT

Let us not sanitize this. Real recovery costs coverage. Removing low-value tasks dents someone's sacred cow. Safer ratios hit the margin unless something else comes off the plate. Grief huddles cost minutes on days you feel like you have none. Peer responder programs need training, supervision, and boundaries to prevent them from becoming unpaid therapy. Privacy is not a poster; It is a design.

You will also run into reflexes built by years of scarcity: "We cannot afford it." "They will take advantage." "If we give an inch…" Sometimes that fear is honest. Respond with the numbers and the names behind them. Disclose what traveler spending looks like next to a two-point improvement in retention. Show how incident reports moved when security walked the lot where the risk lived. Show the difference in after-hours charting when scribes were on. Pair the numbers with a human who stayed because you made one thing easier on a Tuesday.

Furthermore, watch for the traps:

- **Performative care**. Muffins, apps, and platitudes without workload change breed cynicism faster than doing nothing.
- **Leadership whiplash**. Big speeches followed by no budget teach people to keep their heads down.

- **Privacy theater**. Promise confidentiality and then route counseling through a trackable portal? Participation dies.
- **Metric gaming.** If your engagement score becomes the goal, the truth will vanish.
- **Equity theater**. If nights cannot get childcare, if rural sites never see the peer responder, if new parents are given "flexibility" that punishes them, your culture will split along fault lines you claim to care about.

You do not avoid these by being perfect. You avoid them by being explicit. Name the tradeoffs. Publish the rationale. Show the gains. Change course when it does not work. People do not need magic; they need proof.

IF YOU LEAD FROM DIFFERENT SEATS

If you are a CEO, put well-being on the same dashboard as safety, quality, and cost. Tie one budget line to a concrete redesign action each quarter. Show your board the before-and-after. Back your managers when they spend political capital to protect recovery time. Ask about nights and rural sites every time.

If you are a CMO or CNO, teach just culture as you would infection control. Be specific about what gets a coaching conversation and what crosses the line. Protect those who report hazards. Make the "we heard / we did" cadence sacred. Fix one process a month in public.

If you are a manager, learn to run a grief huddle and a two-question check-in. Keep a small list of tasks you can remove when the room is heavy. Write down what you heard and what you changed. Close the loop. Individuals are often more understanding when they observe genuine effort.

If you are a clinician without formal authority, your leverage is truth and example. Model boundaries. Use the red flag pass. Participate in pilots. Normalize help-seeking. The moment you ask for what you need, you permit someone else to do the same.

WHAT SUCCESS FEELS LIKE

It will not look like a banner on the intranet. It will feel like fewer sick calls on Monday after a brutal weekend. It will sound like laughter returning to a team that had gone quiet. It will show up as fewer short-notice resignations, fewer near misses for the same dumb reason, and more hazard reports that are fixable. Families will say, "Care felt calmer." New graduates will stop whispering, "Is it always like this?" and start asking, "Where can I learn more?"

Executives will notice too. Traveling nurses spend softens. Time-to-fill drops a little. Safety events shift from injury to learning. The CFO stops calling well-being "soft" and starts asking which lever moves retention.

Furthermore, you will notice yourself. You will sleep better. You will catch yourself planning next quarter instead of simply bracing for next shift. You will feel proud again in a way that is not hollow.

A BRIEF WORD TO TRAINEES AND THE NEXT WAVE

You were told to demonstrate resilience. You were instructed to work hard. You were handed a pager and an apology. Here is the truth: toughness without recovery is a slow injury. Your job is to learn and to care, not to erase yourself. Ask for the day when you need it. Document the hazard when you see it. If you land in a place that punishes honesty, believe what it tells you and take your talent somewhere that deserves you. You are not asking for favors. You are asking for the conditions that keep patients safe.

ONE LAST PRACTICE THE AFTER-ACTION THAT RESTORES

When you finish a hard month, run a ten-minute "what we will carry forward" huddle:

- Name one fix that worked. Keep it.
- Name one thing you will stop. Kill it for a month.
- Name one support you will protect. Put a date on it.

Three lines on a whiteboard. Owners. Dates. Follow-up. That is how culture moves from sentiment to system.

ONE FINAL CHARGE

Let this be the start of a new chapter, not just for your organization, but for you. We owe this to the people who kept showing up through storms, surges, staffing crises, and the noise of the world. We owe it to the next generation to decide right now whether this field is worth the cost. We owe it to ourselves to stop worshiping exhaustion and start declaring that sustainability is essential.

Survival is not the target anymore. Healing is. Moreover, healing is human first.

There may be a tendency to delay action while awaiting an ideal strategy or the appropriate funding opportunity. Do not. Pick one unit and run a ninety-day pilot. Fix one hazard. Protect one hour. Fund one redesign. Tell the truth every week. Publish what moved. Repeat.

When the room sees a pattern it can predict, leaders tell the truth, fix what is fixable, protect recovery, and share power, the trust returns. Energy follows trust. Safety follows energy. Care follows all of it.

We do not just rebuild systems. We restore people. Furthermore, when we do, the rest of the work becomes possible again.

I wrote this through the lens of Louisiana, a place shaped by storms, resilience, and community—but the truths we have walked through together belong to all of us. I count you as a dear colleague on this journey.

Thank you for standing with me. In Cajun French, we like to say:

"Sois bien, mon ami." *In English, it means,* ***"Be Well, my friend"***

APPENDIX
The Well-Being Implementation Toolkit

FOR HEALTHCARE ORGANIZATIONS IN CRISIS-TESTED SYSTEMS

This toolkit provides actionable resources to support leaders, HR professionals, educators, and wellness champions in integrating well-being into the core of healthcare operations—not as an add-on but as an integral part of the infrastructure.

---

1. **Leadership Audit: 10 Quick Questions to Check** Culture Health

Use these to assess whether your organization supports well-being or unintentionally reinforces burnout.

- ☐ Do leaders openly discuss mental health, stress, and trauma in meetings?
- ☐ Are managers trained in trauma-informed supervision?
- ☐ Do team members feel psychologically safe to say, "I am not okay"?
- ☐ Are there clear pathways for staff to access mental health support confidentially?
- ☐ Are wellness and burnout metrics part of executive dashboards?

- ☐ Is PTO extensively used and respected (i.e., no guilt, no after-hours texts)?
- ☐ Is workload regularly assessed and adjusted based on staffing and acuity?
- ☐ Are there policies in place to support recovery after disaster deployments?
- ☐ Do we regularly discuss mission, values, and purpose in addition to productivity?
- ☐ Are equity and inclusion part of the well-being conversation?

If you answered "no" to three or more, it is time to redesign your approach.

---

2. Emotional Wellness Pulse Check
(Staff Self-Assessment Tool)

Distribute quarterly and following a crisis. This can be anonymous or used for guided 1:1s.
On a scale from 1–10, how would you rate your emotional well-being today?
(1 = Deep distress; 10 = Thriving)
Which of the following have you experienced in the last month?

- ☐ Sleep issues
- ☐ Increased anxiety or irritability
- ☐ Detachment from work
- ☐ Trouble concentrating
- ☐ Physical fatigue or unexplained pain
- ☐ Feeling emotionally numb or withdrawn

□ Thinking of leaving the profession

Optional prompt: What is one thing that would make work more manageable right now?

---

3. Organizational Well-being Red Flags (Post-Crisis Check-In)

Review these signs in leadership teams, HR, or wellness committees:

- Increased sick leave and FMLA requests.
- Resignations within ninety days post-disaster
- Staff complaints about communication, fairness, or lack of support
- The high number of "silent, disengaged" staff—present but checked out.
- Decreased patient satisfaction scores with no clinical explanation.
- Conflict spikes or breakdowns in cross-departmental collaboration
- Emotional reactions surfacing in unrelated meetings or interactions.

Use these as signals to pause, assess, and respond—not power through.

---

4. Healing in Practice: 5 Post-Disaster Recovery Tactics That Work

□ Crisis Debrief Circles

□ Facilitated 30–45-minute reflection spaces for teams after disasters or surges. No agenda. Just presence and permission to process.

□ "Protected Recovery Time" for Frontline Staff

- ☐ After major emergencies, they offer reduced hours, low-acuity assignments, or non-clinical recovery shifts.
- ☐ Peer Support Roster
- ☐ Train peer responders or "emotional first responders" to support colleagues privately after traumatic events.
- ☐ Wellness Grants
- ☐ Provide small funding pools for departments to implement wellness ideas (e.g., mindfulness, massage, snacks, rest pods).
- ☐ Survivor Acknowledgment Ceremonies

After hurricanes, floods, or significant losses, mark survival, honor effort, and grieve together.

---

5. Messaging Templates for Culture Change

For Leaders Talking About Burnout:

"This work is hard. We are not here to pretend it is not. What matters is that we discuss it, support one another, and commit to building something healthier together.

For Setting a New Norm Around Asking for Help:

"Asking for help is not weakness—it is leadership. None of us is above support. If you are struggling, please do not hesitate to speak up. You are not alone."

For New Employee Onboarding:

"Here, we care about your actions, not just what you produce. Well-being is part of your job, and it is part of our culture."

---

6. Your Next 60 Days: Well-being Action Plan

- Weeks 1–2

☐ Distribute Emotional Wellness Pulse Check.

- ☐ Host one sixty-minute Leadership Roundtable on well-being culture gaps.

- Weeks 3–4

- ☐ Launch post-disaster debrief (if applicable).
- ☐ Identify two or three policies that need to shift (e.g., PTO, workload, overtime).

- Weeks 5–8

- ☐ Implement one quick win (e.g., dedicated quiet space, realigned rounding).
- ☐ Communicate a system-wide message from leadership about well-being as a priority.
- ☐ Begin planning long-term infrastructure: budget, metrics, roles.

FINAL NOTE FROM THE AUTHOR

You do not need perfection to start. You need **honesty, intention, and follow-through**.

This work is not about checking a box. It is about creating a culture where people can do meaningful work **without losing themselves**, especially in places like Louisiana, where hardship is frequent, and healing must be intentional.

The resilience is already there. Let us make sure **recovery** is, too.

DISCUSSION GUIDE
Still Standing

PURPOSE OF THIS GUIDE

To foster meaningful conversations, promote personal reflection, and inspire collective action on trauma-informed leadership, workforce well-being, and cultural change in healthcare.

1

When the Next Crisis Hits
Before the Last One Heals

- Which "serial crisis" patterns (human, safety, operational, equity) are most visible on your team?
- What overlap planning (staffing, stockpiles, cross-training) is currently missing?
- What small, paid recovery window would be most protective where you work after critical events?

2

How I Got Pulled
Into the Deep End

- What early-career experience shaped your coping style—for better and for worse?

- Where do informal debriefs already happen, and how could you legitimize them?
- Which distinctions (burnout vs. depletion vs. moral distress vs. moral injury) show up around you?

3

How We Got So Depleted
The Cost of Living in Crisis Mode

- What parts of your "crisis baseline" are now invisible because they feel ordinary?
- Which non-clinical teams are carrying hidden load, and how would you know?
- What one process would you pause for 90 days to buy back recovery time?

4

Beyond the Hospital Wall:
The Unseen Backbone

- Where are Maria and DeShawn in your system—and what do they need first?
- Which disaster-recovery practice (peer debriefs, staffing, equipment) would most reduce churn?
- How could you detect early distress in EMS/LTC/home health without extra paperwork?

5

Beyond Burnout
What Healthcare Can No Longer Ignore

- Where do you see the stress→burnout→trauma continuum

in your people today?
- What would "trauma-informed leadership" change about tomorrow's assignments and huddles?
- How will you surface and address moral distress before it becomes moral injury?

6

Why Recovery Must Follow Resilience

- Where is endurance being mistaken for resilience in your org?
- What is one recovery block you can hard-wire (paid, scheduled, protected) after heavy exposure?
- Which low-value tasks will you drop to fund/cover recovery time?

7

The Silence Behind the Scrubs
Why Do We Not Ask For Help

- Which policies, forms, or unwritten rules make help-seeking risky in your setting?
- How will leaders model care-seeking without tokenism?
- What privacy/credentialing language must change (current impairment vs. lifetime history)?

8

Measuring the Damage
How We Know What We Are Facing

- What is your 2-minute monthly pulse + 10-minute

semiannual tool set—and who sees raw data?
- How will you run the 7-day "we heard → we did" loop so data reliably becomes change?
- Which one safety metric will you pair with well-being trends?

9

What Would It Take to Build Something Better—After Everything

- Where will you share power (budget/time/rules) closest to harm, and how soon?
- Which work-redesign move (EHR relief, role redesign, scribes) would free the most minutes?
- What equity gaps (nights, rural, caregivers) must be built into recovery plans from the start?

10

Leading the Rebuild Tools to Restore Trust, Energy, and Well-Being

- What weekly safety signal/fix would rebuild trust fastest on your unit?
- Who will be trained for grief huddles/PFA, and how will coverage make it possible?
- What cadence of "truth in public" (what is known/unknown/changed/slipped) can you sustain?

11

We Do Not Just Rebuild Systems. We Restore People

- What three visible patterns (truth cadence, hazard fixes, protected recovery) will you make predictable?
- What tradeoffs will you name out loud (and why) to keep trust intact?
- Where will you run your 90-day pilot (unit, owner, measures) and what will "success" feel like?

Appendix – Toolkit for Action

- Which tools in the Well-being Implementation Toolkit would make the most significant difference in your environment?
- What challenges might arise in implementing these tools? How could they be overcome?
- Who needs to be part of the conversation to move from insight to action?

Wrap-Up Reflection Questions

- What did you learn about yourself while reading this book?
- What part of your organization's culture are you most motivated to change?
- How will you carry forward this message of well-being and healing in your work?

About the Author

Laurinda Calongne, EdD, is a healthcare executive, trauma-trained social worker, and medical educator.

Laurinda started her career as a licensed clinical social worker, working in high-intensity settings such as emergency rooms, critical care units, and trauma services. Those early years gave her a close view of human suffering and the systemic barriers that too often compounded it. That perspective shaped the path she would take—moving into academic medicine, guiding leadership development, and advancing graduate medical education.

She has helped transform a community hospital into a nationally recognized academic medical center, led large-scale initiatives on clinician burnout and well-being, and advised national bodies on the future of healthcare training and workforce policy.

However, her most powerful lessons did not come from conferences or board meetings. They came from witnessing burnout up close, from supporting colleagues through hurricanes, COVID surges, and, heartbreakingly, the loss of team members to suicide. Her most provocative leadership lessons came from ensuring that individuals who provide care for others receive adequate care and support for themselves.

Today, she partners with organizations to implement well-being initiatives and designs programs that strengthen workforce recovery and resilience. She teaches and consults on trauma-informed leadership, offers executive coaching to senior leaders, and guides culture change across healthcare organizations. In addition to her coaching practice, she writes and speaks widely on leadership and clinician wellness and is a frequent presenter at national leadership conferences.

BIBLIOGRAPHY

Accreditation Council for Graduate Medical Education. (n.d.). Physician well-being. https://www.acgme.org/what-we-do/initiatives/physician-well-being/

Adler-Milstein, J., & Huckman, R. S. (2013). The impact of electronic health record use on hospital productivity. Health Affairs, 32(11), 1960–1967.

Aiken, L. H., Sloane, D. M., Bruyneel, L., et al. (2014). Nurse staffing and education and hospital mortality in nine European countries. The Lancet, 383(9931), 1824–1830.

Ball, J. E., Bruyneel, L., Aiken, L. H., Sloane, D. M., Rafferty, A. M., Lindqvist, R., … Sermeus, W. (2018). Post-operative mortality, missed care and nurse staffing in nine countries: A cross-sectional study. International Journal of Nursing Studies, 78, 10–15. https://doi.org/10.1016/j.ijnurstu.2017.10.001

American Ambulance Association & Newton 360. (2022). 2022 Ambulance Industry Employee Turnover Study [member report]. Overview: https://ambulance.org/category/human-resources/recruitment-retention/

American Hospital Association. (2023). The cost of violence in hospitals and health systems.

American Medical Association. (2021). AMA STEPS Forward®: Preventing physician burnout. https://edhub.ama-assn.org/steps-forward/module/2702509

American Nurses Foundation. (2021). Pulse surveys of nurses: Mental health & wellness.

Arnsten, A. F. T. (2009). Stress signaling pathways that impair prefrontal cortex structure and function. Nature Reviews Neuroscience, 10(6), 410–422. https://doi.org/10.1038/nrn2648

Bodenheimer, T., & Sinsky, C. (2014). From triple to quadruple aim: Care of the patient requires care of the provider. Annals of Family Medicine, 12(6), 573–576. https://doi.org/10.1370/afm.1713

Brooks, S. K., Webster, R. K., Smith, L. E., Woodland, L., Wessely, S., Greenberg, N., & Rubin, G. J. (2020). The psychological impact of quarantine and how to reduce it: Rapid review of the evidence. The Lancet, 395(10227), 912–920. https://doi.org/10.1016/S0140-6736(20)30460-8

Bureau of Labor Statistics. (2023). Occupational Employment and Wage Statistics (OEWS).

Centers for Disease Control and Prevention, National Center for Health Statistics. (2023). Excess deaths associated with COVID-19. https://www.cdc.gov/nchs/nvss/vsrr/COVID19/excess_deaths.htm

Daugherty Biddison, E. L., Faden, R., Gwon, H. S., Mareiniss, D. P., Regenberg, A. C., Schoch-Spana, M., … Toner, E. S. (2019). Too many patients…A framework to guide statewide allocation of scarce mechanical ventilation during disasters.

CHEST, 155(4), 848–854. https://doi.org/10.1016/j.chest.2018.09.025

Dekker, S. (2017). Just culture: Restoring trust and accountability in your organization (3rd ed.). CRC Press.

Downing, N. L., Bates, D. W., & Longhurst, C. A. (2018). Physician burnout in the electronic health record era: Are we ignoring the real cause? Annals of Internal Medicine, 169(1), 50–51. https://doi.org/10.7326/M18-0139

Dyrbye, L. N., Johnson, P. O., Johnson, L. A., Satele, D., & Shanafelt, T. D. (2020). Efficacy of the Well-Being Index to identify distress and stratify risk of adverse outcomes in nursing home staff. Mayo Clinic Proceedings: Innovations, Quality & Outcomes, 4(3), 248–255. https://doi.org/10.1016/j.mayocpiqo.2020.03.006

Dyrbye, L. N., Satele, D., & Shanafelt, T. D. (2014). Ability of a 9-item Well-Being Index to identify distress and stratify risk among physicians. Journal of Occupational and Environmental Medicine, 56(6), 631–638. https://doi.org/10.1097/JOM.0000000000000175

Dyrbye, L. N., West, C. P., Sinsky, C. A., Goeders, L. E., Satele, D. V., & Shanafelt, T. D. (2017). Medical licensure questions and physician reluctance to seek care for mental health conditions. Mayo Clinic Proceedings, 92(10), 1486–1493. https://doi.org/10.1016/j.mayocp.2017.06.020

Edmondson, A. C. (1999). Psychological safety and learning behavior in work teams. Administrative Science Quarterly, 44(2), 350–383. https://doi.org/10.2307/2666999

Epstein, E. G., & Hamric, A. B. (2009). Moral distress, moral residue, and the crescendo effect. The Journal of Clinical Ethics, 20(4), 330–342.

Federal Emergency Management Agency. (2006). Hurricane Katrina in the Gulf Coast: Mitigation Assessment Team report (FEMA 549). Author.

Gandhi, A., Yu, H., & Grabowski, D. C. (2021). High nursing home staff turnover and quality of care. Health Affairs, 40(3), 384–391. https://doi.org/10.1377/hlthaff.2020.00957.

Greenberg, N., Docherty, M., Gnanapragasam, S., & Wessely, S. (2020). Managing mental health challenges faced by healthcare workers during COVID-19. BMJ, 368, m1211. https://doi.org/10.1136/bmj.m1211.

Halpern, J., Maunder, R. G., Schwartz, B., & Gurevich, M. (2009). Identifying, describing, and expressing emotions after critical incidents in paramedics. Journal of Traumatic Stress, 22(2), 111–115. https://doi.org/10.1002/jts.20403

Han, S., Shanafelt, T. D., Sinsky, C. A., Awad, K. M., Dyrbye, L. N., Fiscus, L. C., Trockel, M., & Goh, J. (2019). Estimating the attributable cost of physician burnout in the United States. Annals of Internal Medicine, 170(11), 784–790. https://doi.org/10.7326/M18-1422.

Hennein, R., & Lowe, S. R. (2020). A hybrid inductive–abductive analysis of health care workers' experiences and well-being during the COVID-19 pandemic. International Journal of Environmental Research and Public Health, 17(22), 9025. https://doi.org/10.3390/ijerph17239025

Jameton, A. (1984). Nursing practice: The ethical issues. Prentice Hall.

Johns Hopkins University. (2021). Coronavirus Resource Center—Louisiana. https://coronavirus.jhu.edu/region/us/louisiana

Keyes, C. L. M. (2002). The mental health continuum: From languishing to flourishing in life. Journal of Health and Social Behavior, 43(2), 207–222.

Knabb, R. D., Rhome, J. R., & Brown, D. P. (2005). Tropical Cyclone Report: Hurricane Katrina, 23–30 August 2005. National Hurricane Center, NOAA/NWS.

Louisiana Department of Health. (2022). Hurricane-related mortality in Louisiana.

Louisiana Recovery Authority. (2007). Health Care Reform for Louisiana: Final Report of the Health Care Reform Panel.

Mantri, S., Lawson, J. M., Wang, Z., & Koenig, H. G. (2020). Identifying moral injury in healthcare professionals: The Moral Injury Symptom Scale–Healthcare Professionals Version (MISS-HP). Journal of Religion and Health, 59(5), 2323–2340. https://doi.org/10.1007/s10943-020-01065-0

Maslach, C., & Jackson, S. E. (1981). The measurement of experienced burnout. Journal of Occupational Behaviour, 2(2), 99–113.

Maslach, C., Jackson, S. E., & Leiter, M. P. (2018). Maslach Burnout Inventory manual (4th ed.). Mind Garden.

Maslach, C., & Leiter, M. P. (2016). Understanding the burnout experience: Recent research and its implications for psychiatry. World Psychiatry, 15(2), 103–111. https://doi.org/10.1002/wps.20311

McEwen, B. S. (2004). Protection and damage from acute and chronic stress: Allostasis and allostatic load. Annals of the New York Academy of Sciences, 1032(1), 1–7.

Mitchell, J. T. (2011). Critical Incident Stress Debriefing (CISD): Group crisis intervention (Rev. ed.). International Critical Incident Stress Foundation.

Morganstein, J. C., & Ursano, R. J. (2020). Ecological disasters and mental health: Causes, consequences, and interventions. Frontiers in Psychiatry, 11, 468. https://doi.org/10.3389/fpsyt.2020.00468

National Academies of Sciences, Engineering, and Medicine. (2019). Taking action against clinician burnout: A systems approach to professional well-being. The National Academies Press. https://doi.org/10.17226/25521

National Academies of Sciences, Engineering, and Medicine. (2022). Building Resilience to Compound Disasters During COVID-19 and Beyond: Proceedings of a workshop—in brief. The National Academies Press. https://doi.org/10.17226/26654

National Academy of Medicine. (2022). National Plan for Health Workforce Well-Being (V. J. Dzau, D. G. Kirch, V. H. Murthy, & T. J. Nasca, Eds.). The National Academies Press. https://doi.org/10.17226/26744

National Oceanic and Atmospheric Administration, National Weather Service. (2017). Service Assessment: August 2016 South-Central Louisiana Floods. (Characterizes event rarity). https://www.weather.gov/media/publications/assessments/16Aug_South_Central_LA_Floods.pdf

National Weather Service. (2017). Service assessment: August 2016 South-Central Louisiana floods. NOAA.

NSI Nursing Solutions, Inc. (2023). NSI national health care retention & RN staffing report.

NSI Nursing Solutions, Inc. (2024). NSI national health care retention & RN staffing report.

Ochieng, N., Gaboda, D., & Hamel, L. (2022). Adverse events in hospitals rose for Medicare patients during COVID-19 surges. KFF Issue Brief. https://www.kff.org/medicare/issue-brief/adverse-events-in-hospitals-rose-for-medicare-patients-during-COVID-19-surges/

O'Connor, P., Byrne, D., & O'Dea, A. (2022). "You do not look like a surgeon": Microaggressions, discrimination, and burnout in medicine—A narrative review. Academic Medicine, 97(11), 1646–1655. https://doi.org/10.1097/ACM.0000000000004862

Occupational Safety and Health Administration. (2023). Workplace violence in healthcare: Understanding the challenge and prevention strategies.

O'Donovan, R., & McAuliffe, E. (2020). A systematic review of factors that enable psychological safety in healthcare teams. BMC Health Services Research, 20, 810. https://doi.org/10.1186/s12913-020-05680-3.

Panagioti, M., Panagopoulou, E., Bower, P., et al. (2017). Controlled interventions to reduce burnout in physicians: A systematic review and meta-analysis. JAMA Internal Medicine, 177(2), 195–205. https://doi.org/10.1001/jamainternmed.2016.7674

Panagioti, M., Geraghty, K., Johnson, J., et al. (2018). Association between physician burnout and patient safety, professionalism, and patient satisfaction: A systematic review and meta-analysis. JAMA Internal Medicine, 178(10), 1317–1331. https://doi.org/10.1001/jamainternmed.2018.3713

Pfefferbaum, B., Blais, A., North, C. S., & Spitznagel, E. L. (2012). Is the prevalence of posttraumatic stress disorder increasing in firefighters? A meta-analysis. Prehospital and Disaster Medicine, 27(6), 523–528. https://doi.org/10.1017/S1049023X12001000

Pfefferbaum, B., & North, C. S. (2020). Mental health and the COVID-19 pandemic. The New England Journal of Medicine, 383(6), 510–512. https://doi.org/10.1056/NEJMp2008017

Porges, S. W. (2011). The polyvagal theory: Neurophysiological foundations of emotions, attachment, communication, and self-regulation. W. W. Norton & Company.

Rudowitz, T., Rowland, D., & Shartzer, A. (2006). Health care in New Orleans before and after Hurricane Katrina. Kaiser Family Foundation.

Substance Abuse and Mental Health Services Administration. (2014). Psychological First Aid: Field Operations Guide (2nd ed.). https://www.nctsn.org/resources/psychological-first-aid-pfa-field-operations-guide

Shanafelt, T. D., Balch, C. M., Bechamps, G. J., et al. (2010). Burnout and medical errors among American surgeons. Annals of Surgery, 251(6), 995–1000. https://doi.org/10.1097/SLA.0b013e3181bfdab3

Shanafelt, T. D., Gorringe, G., Menaker, R., et al. (2015). Impact of organizational leadership on physician burnout and satisfaction. Mayo Clinic Proceedings, 90(4), 432–440. https://doi.org/10.1016/j.mayocp.2015.01.012

Shanafelt, T. D., Hasan, O., Dyrbye, L. N., et al. (2016). Changes in burnout and satisfaction with work–life integration in physicians and the U.S. working population between 2011 and 2014. Mayo Clinic Proceedings, 91(11), 1681–1694. https://doi.org/10.1016/j.mayocp.2016.08.023

Shanafelt, T. D., & Noseworthy, J. H. (2017). Executive leadership and physician well-being: Nine organizational strategies to promote engagement and reduce burnout. Mayo Clinic Proceedings, 92(1), 129–146. https://doi.org/10.1016/j.mayocp.2016.10.004

Shanafelt, T. D., Ripp, J., & Trockel, M. (2020). Understanding and addressing sources of anxiety among health care professionals during the COVID-19 pandemic. JAMA, 323(21), 2133–2134. https://doi.org/10.1001/jama.2020.5893

Shanafelt, T. D., West, C. P., Dyrbye, L. N., et al. (2022). Changes in burnout and satisfaction with work–life integration in physicians during the COVID-19 pandemic. Mayo Clinic Proceedings, 97(12), 2248–2258. https://doi.org/10.1016/j.mayocp.2022.09.002

Sinsky, C., Colligan, L., Li, L., Prgomet, M., Reynolds, S., Goeders, L., Westbrook, J., Tutty, M., & Blike, G. (2016). Allocation of physician time in ambulatory practice: A time and motion study. Annals of Internal Medicine, 165(11), 753–760. https://doi.org/10.7326/M16-0961

Sinsky, C. A., Sinsky, T. A., Rajput, V., & Lynch, D. (2017). Putting "patients over paperwork": Practical steps to team-based care and practice efficiency. AMA STEPS Forward. https://edhub.ama-assn.org/steps-forward/module/2702511

Templeton, K. J., Bernstein, C. A., Sukhera, J., Nora, L. M., Newman, C., Burstin, H., … Bushell, J. M. (2019). Gender-based differences in burnout: Issues faced by women physicians. JAMA Network Open, 2(3), e190096. https://doi.org/10.1001/jamanetworkopen.2019.0096

Tawfik, D. S., Profit, J., Morgenthaler, T. I., et al. (2018). Physician burnout, well-being, and work unit safety grades in relationship to reported medical errors. Mayo Clinic Proceedings, 93(11), 1571–1580. https://doi.org/10.1016/j.mayocp.2018.05.014

Teshome, G., Woldegerima, E., & Hunegnaw, M. (2020). Implementation of brief, structured team debriefs after critical events: A quality improvement report. BMJ Open Quality, 9(4), e001063. https://doi.org/10.1136/bmjoq-2020-001063

Trockel, M., Bohman, B., Lesure, E., Hamidi, M. S., Welle, D., Roberts, L., & Shanafelt, T. D. (2018). A brief instrument to assess both burnout and professional fulfillment in physicians: Reliability and validity, including correlation with self-reported medical errors, in a large physician sample. Academic Psychiatry, 42(1), 11–17. https://doi.org/10.1007/s40596-017-0849-3.

U.S. Government Accountability Office. (2021). Medical supply chain: COVID-19 lessons highlight need for strategic approach to stockpiling (GAO-21-443). https://www.gao.gov/products/gao-21-443

van der Kolk, B. A. (2014). The body keeps the score: Brain, mind, and body in the healing of trauma. Viking.

Willard-Grace, R., Hessler, D., Rogers, E., Dubé, K., Bodenheimer, T., & Grumbach, K. (2014). Team structure and culture are associated with lower burnout in primary care.

Journal of the American Board of Family Medicine, 27(2), 229–238. https://doi.org/10.3122/jabfm.2014.02.130215

Watson, P., Brymer, M., & Bonanno, G. A. (2011). Future directions in disaster mental health: Resilience, resilience trajectories, and interventions. American Journal of Preventive Medicine, 40(5), 620–625. https://doi.org/10.1016/j.amepre.2011.02.019

West, C. P., Dyrbye, L. N., Erwin, P. J., & Shanafelt, T. D. (2016). Interventions to prevent and reduce physician burnout: A systematic review and meta-analysis. Implementation Science, 11(1), 79. https://doi.org/10.1186/s13012-016-0501-7

West, C. P., Dyrbye, L. N., & Shanafelt, T. D. (2018). Physician burnout: Contributors, consequences and solutions. Journal of Internal Medicine, 283(6), 516–529. https://doi.org/10.1111/joim.12752

West, C. P., Dyrbye, L. N., Sinsky, C., & Shanafelt, T. D. (2020). Resilience and burnout: A clarion call to strengthen systems to support clinicians. BMJ, 368, m497. https://doi.org/10.1136/bmj.m497

West, M. A., Eckert, R., Steward, K., & Pasmore, B. (2014). Developing collective leadership for health care. The King's Fund.

White, E. M., Wetle, T. F., Reddy, A., & Baier, R. R. (2021). Front-line nursing home staff experiences during the COVID-19 pandemic. Journal of the American Medical Directors Association, 22(1), 199–203.e1. https://doi.org/10.1016/j.jamda.2020.10.023

World Health Organization. (2024). Mental health at work [Fact sheet]. https://www.who.int/news-room/fact-sheets/detail/mental-health-at-work

Yuma, P. J., Powell, A., Scott, K., & White, K. (2019). Resilience and Coping for the Healthcare Community (RCHC): Development and pilot of a brief intervention for health workers. Journal of Primary Care & Community Health, 10, 1–6. https://doi.org/10.1177/2150132719884189

www.ingramcontent.com/pod-product-compliance
Lightning Source LLC
LaVergne TN
LVHW050916210926
848482LV00012B/456